TIFFANY GOODALL'S
FIRST FLAT
COOKBOOK

The star rating for each recipe in the
book indicates degree of difficulty.

✪ **FOR THE NOVICE COOK**
✪ ✪ **FOR EVERYONE**
✪ ✪ ✪ **FOR THE KEEN COOK**

EDITORIAL DIRECTOR Anne Furniss
ART DIRECTOR Helen Lewis
PROJECT EDITOR Katey Mackenzie
PHOTOGRAPHER Robert Streeter
DESIGNER Katherine Case
PRODUCTION Vincent Smith, Aysun Hughes

First published in 2010 by
Quadrille Publishing Limited
Alhambra House, 27–31 Charing Cross Road,
London WC2H 0LS
www.quadrille.co.uk

Cataloguing-in-Publication Data: a catalogue record for this book is
available from the British Library.

ISBN 978 184400 872 8

Printed in China

INTRODUCTION

"The transition from student at college or university to becoming a young professional, young earner and of course young foodie is the biggest change I have embarked on yet. Gone are the days of student loans, overdrafts, endless lie-ins and the misty morning hangover. Hello to work, earnings, busy life, and responsibility. My first flat was a major milestone in my life.

I moved into my flat last summer and not only was it gut wrenchingly exciting, it was also extremely nerve racking. While at uni I lived in a house of six girls, but now it is just me and another girlfriend. Not so easy to roll over and ignore the council tax papers and bill reminders.

When we first moved in the kitchen was a wasteland. There was zero equipment, nothing, not even a chopping board or frying pan. So not only did I have to shop for food, but I also had to buy some basic kit. But every cloud has a silver lining and that experience prompted me to write this book for others facing the same situation.

So what equipment should you buy, what food should you get in? And if you're about to embark on a 9–5 job or the like, then how is there even time to shop or cook? Follow my tips and you'll find that with a bit of planning you can eat well, save money and consequently really enjoy the precious time you have at home.

You need to be savvy with your budget if you want to eat well. Thrifty is the only way forward. The best place to start saving money is the kitchen. If you follow my tips your food bill will never get out of hand. The trick is not to waste anything. If you've got a bit of leftover chicken don't just think, 'oh this is no good, not much left I'll chuck it.' Cover it and keep it to add to pasta or a delicious chicken salad the next day.

General Kitchen and Shopping Tips

• **ALWAYS** plan your weekly food. I shop on a Monday night after work and buy all the food for the week ahead. This means you can set yourself a weekly food budget and, importantly, stick to it.

• **ALWAYS** have a list to work to when you are shopping. I have seen so many friends just wander aimlessly, picking bits up here and there in the supermarket, and A: the bill is astronomical and B: three quarters end up in the bin.

• **ALWAYS** make use of leftovers. If you're doing a roast at the weekend, shop for all the ingredients you can and get the meat on the day or the day before. Then when planning your next week keep in mind the leftovers from the roast. This rule also applies to unexpected leftovers. So if, for example, you have some leftover breakfast sausages, think about how you can use them to make dinner, such as sausage stew (see pages 56–57).

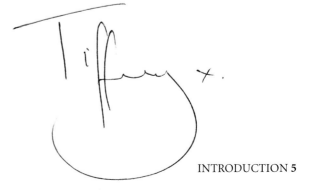

BASIC KITCHEN EQUIPMENT

" A good knife and chopping board are a fantastic investment. Ask for them as a birthday present if funds are tight. If you have lovely things in your kitchen – kit that really works – cooking will be a lot more inviting and a whole load easier. "

Cooking is so much easier when you have an organised kitchen. When I lived with my mum for a bit after uni, she would hide my machines and big chopping boards in the cellar as she thought it was clutter and it drove me mad! Now I know where everything is and even though my kitchen is small I love it as it's just how I want it.

When moving into your home, IKEA do fantastic boxes of starter kit equipment and starter kit crockery for competitive prices. They are fantastic so go in a pair of comfy shoes and muscles at the ready; I bet you'll have a ball collecting things. Saying that, charity shops are brilliant places to pick up quirky kitchen bits, as are the hardware shops you've probably ignored all your life, until now.

When you go on holiday look out for unusual pots and pans. While in Morocco I picked up a tagine for next to nothing, and in Portugal I bought a big pottery bowl perfect for salads. The best thing about having your own place is that you can build up a collection of lovely bits, and every item will mean something to you.

These are the basic bits of kit you'll need:

- Good **wooden chopping board**
- **Fish slice**
- **Hand held whizzer** (for making speedy soup)
- Large **sharp knife** (don't put your knives in the dishwasher or they will become blunt)
- **Ladle**
- **Masher**
- **Measuring jug**
- **Mixing bowls** (stainless steel is great)
- A few **ovenproof dishes** for roasting or gratins
- **Potato peeler**
- Large **roasting tray**
- **Spatula**
- **Wooden spoon**
- **Tongs** (useful for everything and anything)
- **Wire rack** (I thought unnecessary at first but so useful for resting meat and cakes)

STORE CUPBOARD ESSENTIALS

"Your store cupboard is like the petrol for your kitchen – it makes it go! The beauty of a store cupboard is that most ingredients in there can last a long while, although you'll find you'll use your favourites again and again."

I have gradually and slowly built up the contents of my store cupboard. If you have the basics, such as oils and rice, a lot of recipes in this book require you to buy only a few extra ingredients. If I want a quick meal on a Monday evening then I will rootle in my cupboards and rummage in the fridge and use what I have got. A risotto or pasta dish is fantastic to use up leftovers – just add a few store cupboard goodies like rice, pasta and couscous.

I have a very simple blackboard on the wall in my kitchen and make a note on it when I'm running low on my 'magic essentials' as I call them. Then when I hit the shops I'll just whiz in and pick them up – very simple stock rotation. If you haven't got a blackboard then simply bluetak a large piece of paper to the wall in your kitchen and keep a pen nearby.

Here's a list of the magic essentials:

- **Balsamic vinegar**
- **Cannellini beans**
- **Chicken stock** or chicken stock cubes
- **Chickpeas**
- **Coconut milk**
- **Couscous**
- **Eggs**
- **Fish sauce**
- A whole lotta **garlic**
- **Honey**
- **Lentils**
- **Olive oil**
- **Pasta**
- **Basmati rice**
- **Risotto rice**
- **Soy sauce**
- **Sunflower/Vegetable oil**
- **Sweet potatoes**
- **Canned tomatoes**
- **White/Red wine vinegar**
- **White and red onions**

Your first flat is the best place to start building a collection of spices. They can be pricy, but you use so little each time that they last for ages. The impact a little spice can have on a dish can be incomparable. Start off with the following:

- **Cardamom**
- **Cayenne Pepper**
- **Cinnamon**
- **Ground Cumin**
- **Red Chilli Flakes**
- **Turmeric**

1

SOLO SUPPERS

After a long day at work, you need a
quick fix of deliciousness. Soups, salads
and omelettes are brilliant fast food,
and also great for using up leftovers.
Don't hold back just because you're
cooking for one – treat yourself!

HOW TO MAKE SOUP
SPICED PEA AND MINT SOUP ✪✪ SERVES 3–4

SHOPPING LIST

25g/1oz butter
1 small onion, chopped finely
2 garlic cloves, peeled and
    crushed
1 green chilli, deseeded and
    chopped
500g/1lb 2oz frozen peas
900ml/32fl oz vegetable or
    chicken stock
6–8 mint leaves
1 teaspoon sugar
2 tablespoons double cream
1 teaspoon crème fraîche per
    bowl, to serve
3 mint leaves per bowl, to serve
salt and freshly ground black
    pepper

Soup is a thrifty, nutritious and wonderful meal to have in your fridge. Make a big batch and keep the rest for later in the week. Don't be restricted to leek and potato (even though that's a delicious soup). Think above and beyond. Pea and mint make a delicious healthy soup. I love it come summer or winter, but of course with fresh peas it's much more seasonal and delicious in the summer.

1 Heat the butter in a deep saucepan over a medium heat. Then add the onion, garlic, and chilli to soften for 3–4 minutes.

2 Add the peas and mix well until coated in the buttery sauces. Season well.

3 Now add the mint leaves and sugar. Tip the stock into the pan and bring it to the boil. Simmer, uncovered, for about 15 minutes until the peas are soft.

4 Take a hand-held blender and blitz until smooth (if you prefer a chunkier soup then just blitz half of the soup).

5 Mix in the cream and taste, correcting the seasoning if necessary.

6 Serve with a swirl of crème fraîche, some mint leaves and lots of black pepper.

❖**TIFF'S TIPS** This is a great cooling summer dish and on a hot day can even be served cold. If you want to ring the changes, you could try coriander instead of mint, and it's as gorgeous using red chilli as green.

❖**LEFTOVERS** This recipe makes enough soup for 3 or 4 servings. You can keep the leftovers for up to a week in the fridge; just remember to bring the soup back to the boil each time you serve it.

SWEET POTATO AND COCONUT SOUP SERVES 3–4 ✪✪

SHOPPING LIST

2 tablespoons olive oil
1 small red onion, chopped finely
1 garlic clove, peeled and crushed
1 teaspoon red chilli flakes
1 teaspoon turmeric (optional)
1 large sweet potato, peeled and
   chopped
2 carrots, peeled and sliced
1 teaspoon sugar
1 litre/35fl oz chicken stock
200–250ml/7–9fl oz coconut milk
handful coriander, to serve
salt and freshly ground black
   pepper

It's icy cold outside and arctic winds are freezing your bones. What better way to warm up than with a deep soothing bowl of this? With its velvety texture and slight spice, it's my perfect winter warmer.

1 Take a saucepan and add the olive oil. Heat up for a few minutes then add the red onion, garlic and chilli flakes. Cook over a medium heat for 3–4 minutes until soft.

2 Add the turmeric, if using, and the chunks of sweet potato and carrot. Mix well. Season and sprinkle on the sugar. Allow to soften for a few minutes.

3 Now cover with the stock and bring to the boil.

4 Simmer for 20 minutes until the sweet potato is very soft and then blitz with a hand-held blender.

5 Taste and then add the coconut milk, which gives it such a wonderful flavour. Serve with a good handful of coriander leaves on top.

CHORIZO AND RED LENTIL SOUP SERVES 3–4 ✪✪

SHOPPING LIST

2 tablespoons olive oil
1 red onion, chopped finely
2 garlic cloves, peeled and
   crushed
1 teaspoon red chilli flakes
1 red pepper, deseeded and sliced
115g/4oz chorizo, skin removed
   and sliced
250g/9oz red split lentils
1 litre/35fl oz fresh chicken stock
   (see page 113), hot
2 tablespoons crème fraîche
a few coriander leaves, to serve
   (optional)
salt and freshly ground black
   pepper

This is my showstopper – enlivening in summer and warming in winter. With the lentils acting as a fantastic source of protein, it's hearty and nutritious. To ring the changes, add some coconut milk instead of the crème fraîche, or spice it up with a pinch of cayenne pepper.

1 Heat the olive oil in a saucepan over a medium heat for a few minutes, then add the onion, garlic, red chilli flakes and red pepper slices. Cook for 3–4 minutes until soft.

2 Next add the chorizo slices and see before your eyes the colour seeping from the chorizo, turning your soup a brilliant red. Mix well, coating the chorizo in all the flavours, then add the red lentils.

3 Cover with the hot stock and bring to the boil. Simmer for 15–20 minutes. The lentils will puff up and absorb a lot of the stock, so if it needs some more hot water you could add up to 200ml/7fl oz to make it slightly thinner.

4 Blitz it all with a hand-held blender, then add the crème fraîche, stirring well. Taste and season with salt and pepper.

5 Serve garnished with a few leaves of fresh coriander, if you like. I often eat this with some toasted pitta or flatbread.

SHOPPING LIST

1 individual soft goats' cheese
1 teaspoon olive oil, plus extra to drizzle
thyme sprigs
1 tablespoon butter
5 cherry tomatoes, halved
2–3 tablespoons double cream
½ teaspoon whole grain or English mustard
handful of mixed salad leaves
½ teaspoon red wine vinegar

snipped chives, to garnish
salt and freshly ground black pepper

French dressing:
150ml/5fl oz olive oil
3 tablespoons red or white wine vinegar
½ teaspoon Dijon mustard or mustard
  powder
salt and freshly ground black pepper

WARM MELTY GOATS' CHEESE SALAD WITH BURSTING TOMATOES ✪ SERVES 1

"This delicious salad is inspired by the many different versions of the classic French *salade tiède* or 'warm salad'. It's easy to do, looks gorgeous and what's more tastes absolutely amazing."

1 Preheat the oven to 200°C/400°F/Gas Mark 6.

2 Place the goats' cheese on a baking tray, drizzle with olive oil and scatter over the thyme leaves. Put in the oven for 4–6 minutes until they are just beginning to melt.

3 Meanwhile melt the butter in a saucepan and add the tomatoes, season with salt and pepper and cook for 4–5 minutes until soft.

4 Place the warm goats' cheese on a plate. Remove the tomatoes from the pan using a slotted spoon and place on to the plate, keeping the juices in the pan.

5 Add the cream and mustard to the pan, season with salt and pepper and warm for a few minutes.

6 Meanwhile make the French dressing. Whisk the olive oil and vinegar together in a bowl. Now add the mustard and mix well Drizzle the salad leaves with the dressing and set on the plate.

7 Spoon the cream sauce over the goats' cheese and garnish with snipped chives.

❖**LEFTOVERS** The French dressing will keep for up to a week if stored in an airtight container. Don't worry if you don't have an airtight dressing bottle, an old jam jar will work equally well.

❖**VARIATIONS** You could beef this salad up a bit by adding some beetroot, and chopped walnuts would be gorgeous. If you don't have red wine vinegar, white wine vinegar would work just as well.

❖**TIFF'S TIPS** If you want to toast your bread, place the chunks in a preheated oven at 200°C/400°F/Gas Mark 6 for 5–10 minutes until crispy. For a bit of extra oomph add ½ teaspoon of red chilli flakes to the salad.

SHOPPING LIST

1 red pepper
1 celery stick, chopped
½ red chilli, deseeded and chopped finely,
    or ½ teaspoon red chilli flakes
1 large tomato, chopped
½ red onion, sliced
3 anchovies, chopped
1 teaspoon capers (optional)
hunk of leftover or day-old bread,
    such as ciabatta or country loaf, chopped
    into chunks
handful torn basil

Sticky honey, garlic and balsamic dressing:

150ml/5fl oz olive oil
2 tablespoons white wine vinegar
2 tablespoons balsamic vinegar
½ teaspoon Dijon mustard
½ teaspoon runny honey
1 garlic clove, peeled and crushed
salt and freshly ground black pepper

PUNCHY PANZANELLA SALAD ✪ SERVES 1

"Maximum impact from minimal effort – what's not to love about this dish? Cheap, easy and swift to make, this salad can be ready in minutes, perfect when you've had a big day and need food now, now, now! Originally from Tuscany, it's great for using up leftover bread and vegetables."

1 Preheat the grill to high.

2 Whisk all the dressing ingredients together in a bowl. Alternatively, put them in a jar with the lid on and shake well. Taste and season with salt and pepper.

3 Place the red pepper under the grill for 8–10 minutes, turning regularly, until the skin is blistered and charred. Remove it from the grill and tie it up in a plastic food bag for 5–10 minutes; this will make it easy to remove the skin later.

4 Meanwhile place the celery, chilli, tomato and onion in a serving bowl and mix. Add the anchovies and capers, if using, and stir through the bread chunks. Throw in a handful of torn basil.

5 Now take the pepper out the bag and peel the skin off, which should be easy. Use your fingers to remove the seeds and tear the soft pepper into strips. Add the pepper to the salad.

6 Drizzle with a bit of the honey, garlic and balsamic salad dressing and serve. Yummy!

SHOPPING LIST

handful salad leaves
½ cucumber, peeled into ribbons
1 carrot, peeled into ribbons
1 spring onion, chopped finely
handful bean sprouts
150g/5½oz cooked chicken, sliced
  into thin strips
handful coriander leaves
1 teaspoon sesame seeds
  (optional)

Dressing:

2 tablespoons peanut butter
1 tablespoon vegetable oil
1 teaspoon soy sauce
½ teaspoon sweet chilli sauce
juice of 1 lime

STICKY BANG BANG CHICKEN SALAD ★ SERVES 1

“I once had lots of leftover roast chicken and so I whipped up this oriental style salad. Despite being smugly healthy and cheap to make, the colourful ribbons of cucumber and carrot and the sweetly sticky dressing transform leftovers from frugal to fabulous.”

1 On a plate assemble the salad leaves and cucumber and carrot ribbons. Sprinkle the spring onion and bean sprouts over the top.

2 Make the dressing by mixing the peanut butter with the vegetable oil, soy sauce, sweet chilli sauce and lime juice. It should be smooth and wonderfully creamy.

3 Scatter the cooked chicken on top of the salad. Spoon the dressing over the top and finish with the coriander leaves and sesame seeds, if you're using them. How easy is that?

❖**TIFF'S TIPS** Keep this veggie if you like, and make it with lots of crunchy crisp veggies. Alternatively, try it with pork pan-fried with soy sauce, lime and honey. Awesome.

SHOPPING LIST

3 eggs
50ml/2fl oz milk
25g/1oz butter
4 tablespoons pepperonata (see pages 64–5)
handful crumbled goats' cheese or Cheddar
salt and freshly ground black pepper

PEPPERONATA FRITTATA

SERVES 1 ✪ ✪

"A frittata is the Italian way of making an omelette, cooked in a frying pan and finished in an oven or under a grill. Along with this gorgeous pepperonata, it makes a fantastic meal."

1 Preheat the grill to 200°C/400°F/Gas Mark 6.

2 In a mixing bowl mix the eggs and milk together, seasoning well.

3 Take a deep frying pan and melt the butter over a medium heat.

4 Add the egg mixture and keep pushing it to the edge of the pan until it begins to set.

5 When about 5cm/2in of the frittata has begun to set around the edges, add the pepperonata to the centre of the pan and cook for a further 2–3 minutes without mixing it. Then place the pan under the grill for 2–3 minutes. Make sure you leave the handle out of the heat, however.

6 Remove from the grill and scatter with the cheese to give a gorgeous creamy finish. Slice into wedges and serve with a crisp green salad.

❖TIFF'S TIPS My special tip is to use leftover pasta, such as penne, fusilli, or pasta shells. I often have leftover pasta – it's universally known that we all cook more pasta than actually need. But what do you do with it? Now I chuck any leftover fusilli or pasta shells into a frittata.

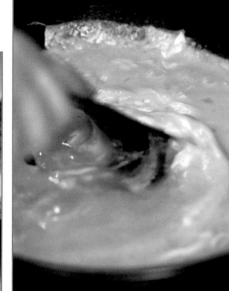

❖LEFTOVERS I usually eat one or two wedges of this frittata and then save the rest for lunch the next day. It's delicious cold and also great as an instant nibble with drinks when you have friends over.

SHOPPING LIST

55g/2oz butter
2 spring onions, chopped
½ teaspoon nutmeg (optional)
150g/5½oz spinach, chopped coarsely
3 eggs
55g/2oz ricotta cheese
2 tablespoons grated Cheddar cheese
sprig of basil, to garnish (optional)
salt and freshly ground black pepper

SPINACH AND RICOTTA OMELETTE **SERVES** 1 ✪✪

❝The trick with omelettes is to let them just flash through the pan so you still get that egg running away off the plate. If you're not a spinach or ricotta fan just make a lovely omelette. Other fillings could be rocket and tomato, or feta and basil. The choice of omelette fillings is endless – think of them as sandwiches.❞

1 Melt half the butter in a frying pan, then add the spring onions and sweat for 2–3 minutes until soft.

2 Add the nutmeg, if using, followed by the spinach, and fry for 2 minutes until soft. Season well. Remove from the pan and set aside.

3 Whisk the eggs in a bowl and crumble in the ricotta. Add the Cheddar cheese and whisk briefly.

4 Go back to the frying pan and melt the remaining butter. Set the heat to high and add the egg mixture. Stir quickly around the pan and then allow to set. This will take 1–2 minutes. Scatter the spinach over the top and leave for 1½ minutes.

5 Tip and fold the omelette onto a plate and serve with a crispy salad.

❖**TIFF'S TIPS** Spinach is full of iron and a natural pick-me-up when you're feeling a bit run down. It's also bang in season from April, so try and use it in abundance then.

❖TIFF'S TIPS If you fancy a healthier approach, skip the frying stage and simply grill for about 5–7 minutes. For an even more indulgent version, however, top with a fried egg. This makes a Croque Madame.

SHOPPING LIST
55g/2oz Gruyère cheese, grated
2 large slices bread, buttered
3 slices good ham
55g/2oz butter
2 tomatoes, quartered
½ red onion, sliced
handful coriander, chopped (optional)
salt and freshly ground black pepper

CROQUE MONSIEUR WITH TOMATO SALAD ✪ SERVES 1

"This is one of my favourite things to have on a Sunday or Monday night if I'm in alone, curled up and watching a film. It's economical and couldn't be simpler. Throw a little tomato salad together for the perfect meal for one."

1 Preheat the grill to hot.

2 Sprinkle the Gruyère cheese on one piece of the buttered bread, then lay the ham slices on top. Season with salt and pepper.

3 Lay the second slice of buttered bread on top of the ham to make a sandwich.

4 Take a heavy pan and melt the butter over a medium heat. Lay the sandwich in the melted butter and fry for a couple of minutes, then turn it over and fry the other side.

5 Slide the sandwich onto a grill pan and transfer it to the hot grill for 4–5 minutes until golden brown and gooey.

6 Meanwhile place the tomatoes and red onion in a bowl and mix well. Add the coriander, if using. Dress with either the French Dressing (see page 14) or the Sticky Honey, Garlic and Balsamic Dressing (see page 17).

7 Remove the Croque Monsieur from the grill and serve with the tomato salad.

SHOPPING LIST

1 small aubergine, sliced
1 beef tomato, sliced, or 4 cherry tomatoes, halved
½ red pepper, deseeded and cut into strips
1 garlic clove, peeled and crushed
1 tablespoon parsley, chopped
1 handful basil leaves, torn
½ teaspoon red chilli flakes
4 tablespoons olive oil
55g/2oz couscous
salt and freshly ground black pepper

GRILLED VEGETABLES WITH HERBY COUSCOUS SERVES 1

For me the best and most instant 'fast' food has to be couscous. Pour boiling water over the couscous and it's ready in a flash. Herby Couscous is also fabulous as part of a summer barbecue. Simply barbecue your summer vegetables and serve them piled high on a glorious bed of fluffy instant couscous.

1 Take a griddle pan and heat it on the hob until really hot. Alternatively preheat your grill to high.

2 Lay the aubergine slices on the grill pan for about 3 minutes each side until they are slightly charred. Remove and set aside.

3 Repeat this with the tomato and red pepper slices.

4 Meanwhile, in a small mixing bowl, mix together the garlic, parsley, basil, chilli flakes and oil. Season really well to make a lovely punchy green salsa.

5 Place the couscous in a bowl and pour in enough boiling water to cover it by 2½cm/1in. Let it sit, covered with a plate, for 5 minutes as it absorbs the water and fluffs up.

6 Fork through the couscous to separate the grains, then spoon in your vegetables and mix through the herby salsa.

7 Pile high and serve.

❖**TIFF'S TIPS** This recipe is a perfect chance to explore your fridge and use spare vegetables. Courgettes work brilliantly, as do red onions, broccoli, any type of peppers; the list is endless. For larger quantities and in the summer this is delicious with a creamy crumbly goats' cheese or even a firmer cheese such as feta.

❖**TIFF'S TIPS** I often make roasted vegetables in bulk and keep them with some olive oil over the top in an airtight container in my fridge. They are marvellous for bruschetta, which is great for weekday nibbles or even a light lunch or supper. They're also brilliant tossed with spaghetti or penne and baked with some cheese on top in the oven. So never ever throw away unwanted vegetables, as this recipe alone will stand you in great stead for the week.

SHOPPING LIST

60g/2½oz rice noodles
1 tablespoon sunflower oil
2 garlic cloves, peeled and crushed
1cm/½inch piece ginger, peeled and chopped finely
1 red chilli, deseeded and chopped finely
1 spring onion, chopped finely
1 teaspoon fish sauce

juice of 1 lime
1 teaspoon granulated sugar
400ml/14fl oz can coconut milk
200ml/7fl oz chicken or vegetable stock (optional)
1 chicken breast, cut into strips
handful of bean sprouts (optional)
handful coriander leaves
lime wedge

CHICKEN AND COCONUT LAKSA SERVES 1 ✪✪

❝Between school and uni I travelled extensively in South East Asia and also visited a cooking school in Chang Mai, northern Thailand for some inspiration. Laksa, a fragrant tasty broth of noodles, is not only fresh and filling but also can be ready in minutes.❞

1 Place your rice noodles in a bowl and cover with boiling water. Cover the bowl with a plate and leave for 5 minutes.

2 Meanwhile, heat the oil in a pan or wok, and when hot add your garlic, ginger, chilli and spring onion. Cook on a medium heat for 1–2 minutes. You don't want them to colour but rather just start to smell fragrant.

3 Add the fish sauce, lime juice and sugar and stir well. Reduce the heat and add the coconut milk.

4 Follow with the chicken, allowing it to slowly poach in the coconut milk for 5–7 minutes until it is tender.

5 Finally add the bean sprouts and cooked rice noodles. Serve sprinkled with coriander and with a wedge of lime.

❖TIFF'S TIPS This is equally delicious with prawns. Cook them in the same way as the chicken strips by poaching them in coconut milk until they turn from grey to pink. This is a perfect dish to pile with veggies such as sugar snap peas, baby corn and spinach for a nutritious feast.

2

10-MINUTE
MEALS

Friends are always saying 'I want to
cook something really delicious but
I haven't got time.' Well this chapter is
for you. Fish can be ready in a flash,
while a speedy stir-fry is as quick
and easy as could be. Throw in a few
seasonal veggies and you're good to go.

HOW TO MAKE HOUMOUS
ORIGINAL HOUMOUS **SERVES 2–4** ✪

SHOPPING LIST
250g/9oz canned chickpeas
2 garlic cloves, peeled
juice of 1 lemon
100ml/3½fl oz tahini paste
3 tablespoons olive oil, plus extra
    to serve
½ teaspoon paprika (optional)
salt and freshly ground black
    pepper

Houmous is a classic Middle Eastern dish and the homemade version is creamy, velvety and a million times more delicious than anything bought in a shop. Serve it with flatbreads, falafel, kebabs or just some simply grilled chicken. Any leftovers can be kept for up to 3 days in an airtight container in the fridge.

1 Drain the chickpeas and place them in a blender.

2 Add the garlic, lemon juice, tahini and olive oil and whiz up. Season well and if it's too thick add about 1 tablespoon water to thin it a bit.

3 Serve on a plate, and I love to drizzle a little olive oil over the top and finish it with a sprinkle of paprika.

ZINGY BROAD BEAN HOUMOUS **SERVES 2–4** ✪

SHOPPING LIST
200g/7oz fresh or canned
    broad beans
250g/9oz canned chickpeas
2 garlic cloves, peeled
juice of 1 lemon
3 tablespoons olive oil
handful basil leaves, chopped
    (optional)
salt and freshly ground black pepper

1 If you're using fresh broad beans, bring a pan of water to the boil and add the beans for 5–6 minutes. Drain them and then peel them or 'pod them'. Some say that they are delicious if you don't do this but I think they have a much brighter zingy colour if you do.

2 Place the beans in a blender with the chickpeas, garlic, lemon juice and olive oil. Whiz them up until smooth, taste and season with salt and pepper.

3 Stir in the chopped basil at the end and serve garnished with an extra sprig.

SPINACH AND FETA HOUMOUS **SERVES 2–4** ✪

SHOPPING LIST
250g/9oz canned chickpeas
2 large handfuls spinach
2 tablespoons tahini paste
2 garlic cloves, peeled
juice of 1 lemon
3 tablespoons olive oil
110g/3¾oz feta cheese, crumbled
salt and freshly ground black
    pepper

1 Drain the chickpeas and put them in the blender.

2 Add the spinach, tahini, garlic, lemon juice and olive oil. Blend till smooth, taste and season with salt and pepper.

3 Mix in the crumbled feta and serve.

SHOPPING LIST

1, 2, 3 or even 4 types of houmous
  (see page 33 and tip, below right)
3 pitta breads
200g/7oz feta cheese
4 tablespoons olive oil
½ teaspoon dried oregano
1 teaspoon ground cumin
100g/3½oz rocket leaves
½ teaspoon red chilli flakes
6 cherry tomatoes, halved
1 teaspoon lemon juice
85g/3oz cold meats, such as Parma or Serrano ham

MY MINI MEZZE ✪✪ SERVES 2–4

❝ Mezze are typically a selection of small bites, perfect to serve with drinks. I tend to throw my mini mezze together if I have a girlfriend round. It's simply a case of assembling it all – the most time-consuming task is making your delicious houmous. ❞

1 Take a large serving platter and spoon the houmous into a serving bowl. Now toast your pitta bread for 3 minutes.

2 Meanwhile place the feta on a plate and spoon over 1 tablespoon of the olive oil, followed by the oregano. Place on your mezze platter.

3 Cut the toasted pitta bread into strips then douse with 2 tablespoons of the olive oil and scatter with the cumin. Place these hot spiced strips on your serving platter.

4 Mix the rocket leaves, chilli flakes and cherry tomato halves together in a bowl. Add the remaining 1 tablespoon olive oil and the lemon juice. Mix well and place on the serving platter. Last, lay the cold meats on the platter as well.

❖**TIFF'S TIPS** This is mezze in a minute, but you can take much more time to expand the selection. Tsatsiki dip is brilliant with this as well. I also love to get some spicy sausages and cook these in oil and serve them hot; it simply depends on how much time and effort you can put in. However, this mini mezze is a great place to start. As the Greeks would say, *yiamas* (cheers!)

❖**BEETROOT HOUMOUS**
Blend two large ready-cooked beetroots and a sprig of rosemary into plain houmous to make a glorious autumnal variation.

SHOPPING LIST

2½cm/1inch piece ginger, peeled and grated
1 garlic clove, peeled and crushed really well
4 tablespoons light soy sauce
1 tablespoon sweet chilli sauce
1 tablespoon light brown sugar
1 teaspoon fish sauce
1 tablespoon lime juice
2 x 115g/4oz salmon fillets
2 tablespoons sunflower oil

BLACKENED THAI GLAZED SALMON SERVES 2 ✪✪

"Salmon is a great fish to start with if you're new to cooking and playing around with fish dishes. The reason for this is that it's packed full of flavour so you don't need to do too much with it to make it taste sensational. This is a sticky nutritious Asian inspired dish."

1 Mix the ginger, garlic, soy sauce, sweet chilli sauce, brown sugar, fish sauce and lime juice in a bowl to make a punchy marinade.

2 Take a brush, or if you don't have one simply use a spoon, and gently brush your marinade mixture all over the salmon, keeping the remaining mixture for the sauce.

3 Heat the oil in a pan over a medium heat. When warm, fry the salmon fillets for 4–5 minutes on each side. Due to the sugar the skin will brown quickly, but don't worry, this adds to the flavour and inside you'll still have a perfectly cooked salmon fillet.

4 Remove the salmon from the pan and leave to rest. Serve with a little of the remaining marinade over the top, if you wish.

5 I love to serve this with simple noodles and a lime wedge on the side, but it doesn't need much as the marinade and salmon have so much flavour going on.

❖**TIFF'S TIPS** This marinade would work as well with prawns and you could serve them with drinks as an easy nibble. Salmon is also beautiful poached in milk or as part of a milky creamy sauce. For a sort of topless fish pie I poach the salmon in some milk and just serve with a creamy cheese sauce and some green vegetables to make a quick and delicious supper.

❖**TIFF'S TIPS** Salmon is a little bit more of a treat but its creaminess works brilliantly with these slightly sweet flavours. When you cut it through the middle after 8 minutes it'll be just perfectly cooked. If you're really hungry and want a more hearty supper, serve it with some penne pasta. This technique would also be ideal when cooking chicken.

❖**LEFTOVERS** Any extra roasted vegetables can do double duty for dinner the following night. Simply toss them through some cooked pasta, drizzle with olive oil, then give it all an extra bit of bite by adding some Parmesan shavings.

SHOPPING LIST

8 cherry tomatoes, halved
1 small red onion, chopped
½ teaspoon red chilli flakes
1cm/½ inch piece ginger, peeled and grated
2 garlic cloves, peeled and bruised
2 tablespoons olive oil
1 x 300g/10½oz fillet of white fish, such as haddock,
     pollack or salmon
juice of 1 lemon
1 teaspoon balsamic vinegar
salt and freshly ground black pepper

MY FISH IN A FLASH ✪ SERVES 1

"Get a roasting tin, chuck in some seasonal vegetables, and lay a piece of fish on top. Add a bit of garlic and a slug of oil and in 8–10 minutes you're laughing. This recipe works wonderfully with pollack, coley or haddock. Coley is a very under-used and thus ethical choice with cod being so over-farmed."

1 Preheat the oven to 200°C/400°F/Gas Mark 6.

2 Place the tomatoes and red onion in an ovenproof dish and sprinkle over the red chilli flakes.

3 Add the ginger and garlic cloves and drizzle over the olive oil. Mix well.

4 Now lay the fish fillet on top of the veggies, skin side down, and season with salt and pepper. Squeeze the lemon over the top. Let the juice run through your fingers so you can catch any pips. Drizzle with the balsamic vinegar, then place in the hot oven for 8 minutes.

5 Remove from the oven and check it's cooked. The flesh should now be opaque.

6 Serve with the roasted veggies. The tomatoes should be soft and bursting. I also like to eat this with a handful of baby spinach leaves and maybe a little French dressing (see page 14).

❖**TIFF'S TIPS** If you're feeling extra hungry top this with a poached egg – absolutely delicious, and rather attractive too. Don't forget, this smart-looking yet economical dish does double duty as a great starter when you have friends over.

SHOPPING LIST

1 tablespoon butter, plus extra to spread
1 garlic cloves, crushed
1 small red onion, chopped finely
2–3 field mushrooms, sliced
2 slices of brown bread
handful of baby spinach leaves
salt and freshly ground black pepper

MAGIC MUSHROOMS ON TOAST WITH SPINACH ⊛ SERVES 1

"You're feeling tired and that takeaway menu is looking quite attractive. *Resist* and try this. There is nothing quite like buttery mushrooms on toast, and when served with wilty spinach they transform into something that is so much more than the sum of its parts. I use woody field mushrooms but of course chestnut or button will work brilliantly too.""

1 Heat a pan with the butter and when melted add the garlic and red onion and sweat for about 3 minutes until soft.

2 Then up the heat and add the sliced field mushrooms. It will look like a good bit of mushrooms at first but then they really shrink, so no worries. Season them well and fry for 4–5 minutes until cooked. They should be soft but slightly crispy.

3 Meanwhile toast and butter your bread.

4 Place the spinach leaves on top of the buttered toast and then spoon the mushrooms over the top. You'll be amazed how quickly the spinach wilts and soaks up all the delicious mushroom juices. Eat immediately.

SHOPPING LIST

4 tablespoons plain flour

1 teaspoon salt

2 teaspoons red chilli flakes

300g/10½oz sirloin or rump steak, cut into strips

5 tablespoons sunflower or vegetable oil

½ head of broccoli, divided into florets

55g/2oz French beans

4 tablespoons soy sauce

1 tablespoon honey

juice of 1 lime

1 tablespoon sesame seeds

CRISPY SIZZLING BEEF STIR-FRY ✪✪ SERVES 2

"My dad is a passionate Chinese food lover, but he always over-orders. There is something about stir-fries at a good Chinese restaurant: the meat is succulent, crispy and tender. My secret – keep your vegetables punchy crunchy."

1 Mix the plain flour, salt and red chilli flakes together in a shallow bowl. For a less spicy version, just use 1 teaspoon of the flakes. Dunk the beef strips in the flour, coating them well and shaking off the excess.

2 Take a frying pan or wok and add the oil. Let it get really hot so it's smoking, but always be careful of hot oil.

3 Now carefully add the chilli beef strips and fry for about 4 minutes until they are crispy and golden.

4 Remove the beef with a slotted spoon and set aside. Next add the broccoli florets and French beans to the hot oil and stir-fry for 2 minutes.

5 Now add the soy, honey and lime juice. Stir-fry for a further 1–2 minutes. The vegetables should be really crispy and delicious.

6 Put the beef back into the pan, sprinkle with the sesame seeds, and serve.

❖**TIFF'S TIPS** This is a fantastic dish that can be served either on its own or with some thin crispy noodles or just some simple fluffy coriander rice. If you're a fan of oyster or hoi sin sauce then chuck some into your stir-fry too.

❖**LEFTOVERS** Serve cold the next day, maybe as a packed lunch to take to work. Add some pre-cooked noodles and a last-minute drizzle of soy sauce for a sticky, sizzly, cold work lunch.

❖**TIFF'S TIPS** I love to be extra cheesy and add little pieces of chopped mozzarella to the grated cheese topping.

SHOPPING LIST

250g/9oz penne pasta
2 tablespoons olive oil
1 red onion, chopped finely
1 red chilli, deseeded and chopped finely
2 garlic cloves, crushed
200g/7oz pancetta cubes or bacon lardons
400g/14oz canned chopped tomatoes
100g/3½oz mascarpone
3 tablespoons chopped parsley
100g/3½oz Gruyère cheese, grated
salt and freshly ground black pepper

AMATRICIANA PENNE PASTA BAKE **SERVES 2** ✪✪

"This is a great twist on the classic Amatriciana sauce and it is a great speedy supper. I use mascarpone to make it slightly more indulgent, and grilling it for a bit adds that great crispiness on top. It's perfect just to throw together, as onions, garlic, canned tomatoes and pasta are pretty much universal kitchen staples."

1 Preheat the grill to hot.

2 Bring a saucepan of water to the boil. Add the penne pasta and cook for 6–8 minutes, according to the packet instructions.

3 Meanwhile make the amatriciana sauce. Drizzle the olive oil into a pan and when warm add the onion, chilli and garlic to soften for about 2–3 minutes. Then increase the heat and add the pancetta cubes. Fry for a couple of minutes until crispy.

4 Now add the tomatoes and season well. Simmer for a few minutes, then stir in the mascarpone and parsley.

5 Drain the penne and add it to the amatriciana sauce. Stir well, taste and season.

6 Tip it all into an ovenproof dish and sprinkle the grated cheese over the top. Place under the hot grill for 3–5 minutes until golden.

7 Serve with a lovely crisp salad and dive in. Heaven.

250g/9oz dried farfalle
1 courgette, peeled
2 tablespoons olive oil
1 green chilli, deseeded and sliced
1 spring onion, chopped
1 teaspoon lemon juice
200g/7oz feta cheese, crumbled
1 tablespoon mascarpone cheese (optional)
Parmesan cheese, grated, to serve (optional)
handful pine nuts, chopped (optional)
salt and black pepper

FARFALLE WITH GRILLED COURGETTE AND FETA

SERVES 2 ✪ ✪

" Courgette is a summer vegetable and part of the squash family. Its most noticeable feature is its blooming orange flower, which at Ballymaloe we used as a garnish for a lot of gorgeous dishes. This recipe would also work well with butternut squash, which could be a great option for winter as it's bang in season then. "

1 Bring a pan of water to the boil and drop in the farfalle to cook for 8–10 minutes, or according to the packet instructions.

2 Meanwhile heat the grill and place the courgette strips in the grill pan. Drizzle with about 1 teaspoon of the olive oil and sprinkle with salt. Place under the grill till slightly curling at the edges and golden. This should take about 4 minutes for each side – do keep a close eye on them.

3 Drain the cooked pasta and return it to the pan over a low-medium heat. Throw in the chilli, spring onion, lemon juice and remaining olive oil and gently stir in the courgette strips. Scatter the feta cheese over the top and season with salt and pepper.

4 If you're using the mascarpone cheese. Fold this in at this stage. Grate a little Parmesan over the top, sprinkle with pine nuts, if you wish, and serve.

❖**TIFF'S TIPS** Try this dish with mozzarella instead of feta. Penne would also be a delicious alternative to farfalle.

❖**LEFTOVERS** Transform leftovers into a pasta bake the next night. Add some tuna and a bit more mascarpone. Top with breadcrumbs and cheese and bake in an oven-proof dish at 180°C/350°F/Gas Mark 4 for 15 minutes.

3

TIFF'S
TUESDAYS

Tuesday night is a great evening to
entertain. If you're organized, dishes like
Veggie Lasagne, and Bloody Mary Cottage
Pie can be made ahead on Sunday
evening and then just popped into the
oven when your guests arrive on Tuesday.
Alternatively, just sip the evening away
chatting and stirring a creamy risotto.

HOW TO MAKE RISOTTO
MELLOW PUMPKIN AND
SAGE RISOTTO SERVES 4 ✪ ✪ ✪

SHOPPING LIST
800ml/28fl oz chicken or
    vegetable stock
2 tablespoons olive oil,
    plus extra to serve
2 garlic cloves, peeled and
    crushed
½ small onion, peeled and
    chopped finely
6–8 sage leaves, chopped finely,
    plus extra to garnish
300g/10½oz arborio rice
1 glass of white wine (optional)
1 butternut squash or pumpkin,
    peeled and roughly diced
1 tablespoon butter
2 tablespoons grated Parmesan
    cheese
sage leaves, to garnish
salt and freshly ground black
    pepper

Risotto rice is a fantastic staple to have in your cupboard. The chances are you'll always have some stock cubes and a splash of leftover wine – then you can just throw all sorts into your risotto, depending on what you have lurking in your fridge. There are three seasonal options, which you can of course adapt as you wish. This pumpkin and sage version is perfect for autumn.

1 Bring the stock to the boil and then keep it at a low simmer while cooking the risotto.

2 In a separate pan heat the oil and when warm add the garlic and onion, followed by the sage leaves. Stir and then leave to sweat until soft – this should take about 5 minutes on a low heat.

3 Increase the heat a little and add the arborio rice, then the white wine, if you're using it, and keep stirring until it is absorbed. Add the cubed squash and a ladleful of stock, and stir again until absorbed. Keep doing this for about 20 minutes until the rice has expanded and is soft and creamy. Taste and season with salt and pepper.

4 Now add the butter and Parmesan. Turn the heat off and let it sit for a couple of minutes while the cheese and butter melt.

5 Serve drizzled with olive oil and garnished with some fresh sage leaves.

OVEN-DRIED TOMATO AND MASCARPONE RISOTTO SERVES 4 ✪✪✪

SHOPPING LIST

250g/9oz cherry tomatoes, halved

4 tablespoons olive oil, plus extra to serve

800ml/28fl oz chicken or vegetable stock

2 garlic cloves, peeled and crushed

1 small red onion, chopped finely

rosemary sprig, chopped

½ teaspoon red chilli flakes

300g/10½oz arborio rice

1 glass of white wine (optional)

125g/4½oz mascarpone

1 tablespoon butter

2 tablespoons grated Parmesan cheese, plus shavings to serve

rocket leaves, to serve

salt and freshly ground black pepper

This is zingy and delicious. You can preserve any extra oven-dried tomatoes for up to a month by keeping them in a jar with oil and maybe some herbs.

1 Preheat the oven to 150°C/300°F/Gas Mark 2.

2 Place the tomatoes in an ovenproof dish and drizzle with half the olive oil. Put in the oven for 30 minutes until dry but still soft. Then remove and set aside.

3 Bring the stock to the boil and then keep at a low simmer while cooking the risotto.

4 In a separate pan heat 2 tablespoons of olive oil. Add the garlic and red onion, followed by the rosemary and chilli flakes. Stir and then leave to sweat until soft – about 5 minutes on a low heat.

5 Increase the heat a little and add the arborio rice, then the white wine, if you're using it, and keep stirring until it is absorbed. Then add a ladleful of stock and stir again until absorbed. Keep doing this for about 20 minutes until the rice has expanded and is soft and creamy. Taste and season with salt and pepper.

6 Fold in the dried tomatoes, mascarpone, butter and Parmesan. Turn the heat off and let it sit for 2 minutes. Serve with rocket leaves and Parmesan shavings.

COMFORTING SMOKED HADDOCK AND POACHED EGG RISOTTO SERVES 4 ✪✪✪

SHOPPING LIST

2–3 smoked haddock fillets, chopped into chunks

400ml/14fl oz milk

800ml/28fl oz chicken stock

2 tablespoons olive oil

2 garlic cloves, peeled and crushed

3 spring onions, chopped finely

2 thyme sprigs, chopped finely

300g/10½oz arborio rice

1 glass of white wine (optional)

juice of 1 lemon

1 tablespoon butter

2 tablespoons grated Parmesan cheese

parsley, chopped

4 eggs

salt and freshly ground black pepper

1 Place the haddock fillet chunks in a saucepan and cover with milk. Season and simmer over a low heat for 10–15 minutes until soft. Remove and set aside.

2 Bring the stock to the boil and then keep at a low simmer.

3 In a separate pan heat the oil and when warm add the garlic, spring onions and thyme. Stir and then leave to sweat until soft – about 5 minutes on a low heat.

4 Increase the heat a little and add the arborio rice, then the white wine, if you're using it, and keep stirring until it is absorbed. Then add a ladleful of stock and stir again until absorbed. Keep doing this for about 20 minutes until the rice has expanded and is soft and creamy. Taste, season and add the lemon juice.

5 Gently fold the flakes of smoked haddock into the risotto, and then the butter, Parmesan and parsley. Turn the heat off and let it sit for a couple of minutes.

6 Bring a frying pan of water to the boil. I find frying pans are much better than saucepans when poaching eggs. Gently break the eggs into the boiling water and cook on high for 1 minute. Then turn the heat down and simmer for 3 minutes. Remove with a slotted spoon and place on the risotto. Season and serve.

SHOPPING LIST

6–8 chicken thighs
1 carrot, peeled and chopped roughly
1 onion, peeled and chopped roughly
1 litre/35fl oz chicken stock
1 glass white wine
400g/14oz puff pastry (if frozen leave it to thaw out for 1–2 hours until soft)
1 egg
salt and freshly ground black pepper

Sauce:

150g/5oz butter
2 onions, peeled and chopped
1 red pepper, deseeded and sliced finely
250g/9oz bacon lardons or pancetta cubes
2 garlic cloves, peeled and crushed
1 tablespoon plain flour
200ml/7fl oz double cream

OMA'S CHICKEN PIE SERVES 6 ✪✪✪

"Oma is my wonderful grandmother and her recipe for chicken pie is without a doubt one of my favourites. There is something amazing about a mother's cooking when you come home, but a grandmother's is truly epic. Although it requires a little more time than other recipes, it is beyond comforting and utterly delicious, so give it a try."

1 Set the oven to 180°C/350°F/Gas Mark 4.

2 Place the chicken thighs in a large saucepan. Add the carrot, onion, chicken stock and wine. Bring to the boil, then reduce to simmering point. Cover with a lid and simmer for 20 minutes.

3 Remove the chicken from the pan and set on a plate to cool. Turn up the heat and simmer the liquid left in the pan for 5–10 minutes. This will thicken the sauce slightly to leave you with about 600ml/ 1 pint cooking juice. Strain the sauce into a bowl and set aside.

4 Put a saucepan over a low heat, melt the butter and add the onions, red pepper, bacon, and garlic. Stir for 5–10 minutes until softened. Stir in the flour and season well with salt and pepper.

5 Grab your chicken juice that you set aside earlier and pour it onto the softened vegetables. Add a little more flour if it's too thick or more water if too thin. It should be thick enough to coat the back of a spoon. Now pour in the cream and stir well. Taste and season – you should have a delicious sauce.

6 Now back to the chicken thighs – tear off all the meat, scatter it into a deep ovenproof dish and pour in your delicious sauce.

7 You can of course leave it like this with no pastry; however, ready-made puff pastry is available in supermarkets. Just cover your dish in a sheet of puff pastry and trim off the extra by running a knife round the outside of the dish – seriously simple.

8 Whisk the egg and brush over the pastry to give a nice shine. Put into the oven for 40–45 minutes and then serve. Your pastry should have puffed up beautifully and be golden and crisp.

❖**TIFF'S TIPS** This is so gorgeous and easy to make and I just adore this type of slow good comfort food. I love it with buttered broccoli and peas. Also you can always keep it as just a veggie pie or even make it a ham or beef pie. Feel free to play around.

❖**SERVING SUGGESTIONS**
Mashed potato, broccoli, peas or just on its own. Enjoy!

❖**LEFTOVERS** This freezes very well for up to a month, or it's lovely for lunch on a crispy oiled ciabatta half with some rocket and basil over the top. You could also blitz it, add some hot stock and make a delicious soup.

SHOPPING LIST

4 tablespoons olive oil

6–8 sausages

1 red onion, chopped finely

3 garlic cloves, peeled, bruised but left intact

1 red chilli, deseeded and chopped finely

150g/5½oz pancetta/bacon lardons (optional)

1 bunch of thyme, rosemary or both

350g/12oz canned cannellini beans

800g/1lb 12oz canned tomatoes

1 glass red wine

1 teaspoon sugar

basil leaves, to serve

salt and freshly ground black pepper

HEARTY SPICED BEAN STEW WITH SAUSAGE SERVES 4 ✪✪

"I tend to make this on a Sunday evening using leftover sausages from Sunday brunch. I just throw in what I want and keep it in the fridge for mid-week get-togethers. Beans are so healthy that's it's hard not to feel just a little bit virtuous, no matter how much red wine is consumed..."

1 Take a heavy frying pan and add 2 tablespoons of the oil. When hot, fry the sausages for 5–8 minutes until golden brown and then set aside on a plate.

2 Wipe the pan clean and then add a splash of the remaining olive oil. Add the red onion, garlic, and red chilli, and soften over a medium heat for 4–5 minutes. Increase the heat and then add the pancetta or bacon lardons, if you're using them. Fry for 3–4 minutes until soft and slightly crispy.

3 Now add the thyme and/or rosemary, cannellini beans, tomatoes, red wine and cooked sausages. Add the sugar and season well.

4 Cover and cook for 1–2 hours on a very low heat. Just 1 hour is fine, but if you have the time 2 hours just matures and strengthens the flavours.

5 Serve with mash or pasta, for example fusilli, gigli or even tagliatelle. Serve with some lovely basil leaves on top.

SHOPPING LIST

2 tablespoons sunflower oil
1 onion, chopped finely
1 red chilli, deseeded and
   chopped finely
2 garlic cloves, crushed
½ teaspoon cumin
½ teaspoon ground coriander
½ teaspoon cayenne pepper
6 cardamom pods, podded and
   crushed

1 large sweet potato, peeled
   and diced
250g/9oz canned red split lentils
1 cinnamon stick (optional)
1 litre/35fl oz chicken stock
200ml/7fl oz coconut milk
salt and freshly ground black
   pepper
parsley sprigs, to garnish

SWEET POTATO AND RED LENTIL CURRY

SERVES 4
★ ★

"This curry uses one of my favourite ingredients: sweet potatoes. Their sweet velvety flavour works so well with coconut milk. They are typically pinky-orange inside although the Boniato variety has a creamy coloured flesh. They also make a delicious mash and sweet potato chips are fab."

1 Heat the oil in a wok and add the onion, chilli and garlic, followed by the cumin, coriander, cayenne pepper and cardamom. Sweat until soft, about 4 minutes.

2 Now add the sweet potato dice and lentils, mix well and leave for a minute or so to absorb the flavours. Throw in the cinnamon stick, if you're using it, and add the chicken stock.

3 Bring to the boil and simmer for about 15 minutes until the potato and lentils are cooked.

4 The lentils absorb a lot of the liquid as they fluff up when cooked. Now stir in the coconut milk and season to taste.

5 Spoon into bowls and garnish with a sprig of parsley. For a delicious supper serve with naan or buttered rice. A few good dollops of yoghurt and mango chutney will help to temper the spicy heat.

❖**TIFF'S TIPS** This can also be a totally delicious soup and I tend to raid my vegetable drawers to see what's leftover; broccoli, carrots, you name it and throw them in with the sweet potato. Add a little bit more liquid if necessary after it has all boiled up and then blend for a delicious nutritious soup.

❖**LEFTOVERS** If you have a drinks party coming, serve this curry on Chinese spoons as a spicy canapé. You can buy them very cheaply or do as I do and borrow some from your local takeaway. Place the spoons on a plate with some of this on them. Add some soured cream and coriander to make a very easy and innovative canapé. Regular tablespoons also work well.

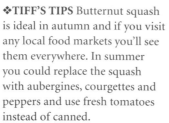

❖**TIFF'S TIPS** Butternut squash is ideal in autumn and if you visit any local food markets you'll see them everywhere. In summer you could replace the squash with aubergines, courgettes and peppers and use fresh tomatoes instead of canned.

❖**LEFTOVERS** You could add this as a sauce for a sweet potato and red lentil curry. It freezes brilliantly, so try freezing it for a month and then pull it out and serve it when you have friends over.

SHOPPING LIST

1 butternut squash, halved
   and deseeded
2 tablespoons olive oil
1 garlic clove, peeled and crushed
1 onion, chopped finely
2½cm/1inch piece of ginger,
   peeled and grated
300g/10½oz red lentils
1 teaspoon ground cumin

½ teaspoon turmeric
½ teaspoon ground cinnamon
½ teaspoon paprika
1x 400ml/14fl oz can coconut milk
400g/14oz canned tomatoes
750ml/26fl oz vegetable or chicken stock
salt and freshly ground black pepper
handful coriander leaves, to garnish
soured cream, to serve

CRESS' BUTTERNUT AND COCONUT DHAL ✪✪ SERVES 4

❝ My friend Cress, who I have known since we were about three, makes this unbeatable dhal. Dhal is a stew of pulses and spices and is native to India and Nepal. When I went to India every dhal seemed different, depending on the pulses and vegetables used. The key is to include the spices – they are slightly expensive but they are an investment because you use such a small amount and they last ages. ❞

1 Preheat the oven to 200°C/400°F/Gas Mark 6.

2 Place the halved squash in a baking tin and drizzle with 1 tablespoon of olive oil. Put in the oven for 30–40 minutes.

3 Meanwhile heat the remaining tablespoon of olive oil in a saucepan and add the garlic, onion and ginger and cook on a medium-low heat until soft.

4 Pour in the red lentils and stir in the spices, mix well and season. Then pour in the coconut milk, tomatoes and stock. Cover and simmer gently for about 30 minutes until the lentils become soft. (If it gets dry add a little hot water, up to 200ml/7fl oz.)

5 Remove the squash from the oven and leave it to rest for a few minutes to cool. Then, using a knife and fork if needed, peel away the skin and tear the flesh into chunks.

6 Add the butternut squash to the cooked lentils. Mix well and season with salt and pepper.

7 Now spoon into warm bowls and top with some coriander leaves and soured cream. Serve with naan bread and rice. Comforting and utterly delish.

SHOPPING LIST

250g/9oz dried lasagne sheets
1 quantity of Tiff's pepperonata
   (see pages 64–5)
100g/3½oz Cheddar or
   Gruyère cheese, for topping
salt and freshly ground black
   pepper

Béchamel sauce:
55g/2oz butter
55g/2oz flour
600ml/21fl oz milk
1 teaspoon English or
   wholegrain mustard
150g/5½oz grated Cheddar
   or Gruyère cheese

Magic mushroom sauce:
75g/2½oz butter
2 spring onions
1 garlic clove, peeled and crushed
400g/14oz mushrooms, sliced
300ml/10½fl oz crème fraîche
juice of 1 lemon

VEGGIE LASAGNE WITH PEPPERONATA AND MAGIC MUSHROOMS SERVES 4 ✦✦✦

"This lasagne is one of the few vegetarian meals that boys eat without asking where the meat is, as it's just utterly delicious. You can make all the elements in advance and keep them separately or make the whole thing and then just bung it in the oven when people come."

1 Prepare the three elements separately: béchamel sauce, pepperonata, and magic mushroom sauce. First the béchamel – melt the butter and then stir in the flour to make a roux.

2 Pour in the milk and whisk slowly over a gentle heat. As the flour starts to cook out you will see the milk thicken. Add the mustard and season really well. It's ready when it's thick enough to coat the back of a spoon. Remove from the heat and stir in the grated cheese. This will melt into the sauce.

3 Next make the magic mushroom sauce. Melt the butter in a pan, then throw in the spring onions and garlic to soften for 2–3 minutes. Add the mushrooms, up the heat and cook for 5 minutes.

4 Now add the crème fraîche and lemon juice. Season to taste, then set aside.

5 Butter the base of an ovenproof lasagne dish, season and then lay some of the lasagne sheets on the bottom, cracking the sheets to fill in the holes, if necessary.

6 Now spoon over 3 tablespoons béchamel sauce and top with 3 tablespoons pepperonata, seasoning each layer.

7 Cover with another layer of lasagne sheets, then add 4 tablespoons magic mushroom sauce. Cover with 3 tablespoons béchamel sauce. Cover with lasagne sheets, and then the rest of the pepperonata and mushrooms. Add another layer of pasta and spoon the rest of the béchamel sauce over the top. This is the final layer, so sprinkle some grated cheese on the top and either leave until you're ready to cook it or bung it in your preheated oven and cook for 30–40 minutes. When ready the pasta will be soft if pricked and the top will be bubbly and golden.

❖**TIFF'S TIPS** Lasagne is a dish that people earmark as just having the traditional beef mince sauce. However, you can pack the layers bursting full with anything from chicken to pork or a selection of vegetables, and it's a great way to use up leftovers, so keep an open lasagne mind!

❖**LEFTOVERS** Leftover béchamel sauce is just brilliant to keep for creating a simple meal. Try it with some ham – very retro and also very delicious.

❖**TIFF'S TIPS** This keeps for about a week if covered tightly in the fridge. It can also be frozen for up to a month. To reheat it, cook until hot in a saucepan.

❖**LEFTOVERS** Spatchcock a chicken by cutting the backbone out and roasting with garlic and lemon. Serve with pepperonata glooped over it as a summery Italian roast chicken.

SHOPPING LIST

2 tablespoons olive oil
2 garlic cloves, peeled and crushed
1 small red onion, chopped finely
2 red peppers, deseeded and sliced
1 yellow pepper, deseeded and sliced
6 tomatoes, diced
1 teaspoon sugar
1 teaspoon red wine vinegar
2 thyme sprigs (optional)

TIFF'S PEPPERONATA ✪✪ SERVES 4–6

"This is a traditional Italian stew based on onions and sweet peppers. I like to add chorizo, pepperoni and other different elements to it, just to ring the changes. It's a ridiculously versatile dish and can be folded though fresh pasta or served with a summer roast chicken. Add chorizo or pancetta to zazz it up a bit."

1 Heat the olive oil in a saucepan and when warm add the garlic and onion. Sweat for 3–4 minutes until soft.

2 Now add all the pepper slices and again sweat gently until soft, about 5 minutes.

3 Now add the tomatoes and sugar, along with the red wine vinegar, and the thyme, if using. Cover with a lid and let it cook very gently for about 30 minutes.

4 Now either serve as part of a pasta dish (such as the Veggie Lasagne on pages 62–3), or spoon it on top of bruschetta or even inside an omelette.

SHOPPING LIST

2 tablespoons olive oil
3 garlic cloves, peeled and crushed
1 red chilli, deseeded and chopped finely
1 red onion, peeled and chopped finely
2 celery sticks, chopped finely
500g/1lb 2oz lean beef mince
2 tablespoons Worcestershire sauce
2 teaspoons Tabasco sauce
1 shot vodka
700g/1lb 9oz passata

pinch celery salt (optional)
salt and freshly ground black pepper

Potato topping:
600g/1lb 5oz floury potatoes, such as
    Maris Piper, peeled and chopped
115g/4oz butter
90ml/3fl oz milk
500g/1lb 2oz grated Cheddar cheese

TIFF'S BLOODY MARY COTTAGE PIE ⭐⭐ SERVES 4–6

"I could rave about this dish and felt quite cool when I thought of it. It's a classic with a twist and sorts a persistent hangover out perfectly. I love it on weekends, ideally with a robust red wine – it's classic comfort food."

1 Preheat the oven to 180°C/350°F/Gas Mark 4.

2 Heat the olive oil in a large saucepan over a medium heat and then add the garlic, chilli, onion and celery. Fry gently for a few minutes until soft. Up the heat, add the mince and cook for 4–5 minutes.

3 Mix together the Worcestershire sauce, Tabasco, vodka, passata and celery salt (if you have some, but leave it out if not). Pour onto the mince and season well.

4 Reduce the heat to a low bubble and cook for 1 hour, or more if you have time. It should taste meaty and delicious.

5 While that is bubbling away, bring a large pan of water to the boil and add the potatoes. Cook until soft, around 15–20 minutes, depending on how small you cut them.

6 Drain and mash well, add the butter and milk and season with salt and pepper. Add half the Cheddar cheese to the hot mash – it will melt and become gorgeously cheesy.

7 Spoon the meat sauce over the bottom of a large ovenproof dish. It should fill half the depth of the dish. Carefully spoon the mashed potato over the top. Season, then sprinkle with the remaining grated Cheddar cheese.

8 Place on a baking tray in the oven for 30–40 minutes until golden and bubbling.

❖**TIFF'S TIPS** This is great to make in advance and freeze uncooked. Make sure you cool the whole dish completely before freezing. It will keep in your freezer for a month. Defrost it thoroughly before popping it into the oven for 40 minutes.

❖**OPTIONAL EXTRAS** For a different version of this dish you could use easily use lamb mince – particularly good if you have some leftover roast lamb. Peel it off the bone, bung it into a food mixer and you'll have lots of delicious lamb to use in your pie.

1.5kg/3lb 5oz belly of pork, ribs still on (optional)
1 tablespoon Chinese five spice
1 teaspoon red chilli flakes
1 teaspoon black pepper
1 teaspoon sugar
2 cloves garlic, peeled and crushed
3 tablespoons vegetable oil
sea salt

MY SPICY STYLE
BELLY OF PORK ✪✪✪ SERVES 4

"Belly of pork is an amazingly low-cost yet delectable cut. In general it's considered quite fatty, which is why it should be cooked longer in order for the fat to be rendered down. The subsequent flavour is extraordinary."

1 Preheat the oven to 220°C/425°F/Gas Mark 7.

2 Take an extremely sharp knife and with a good bit of elbow grease slit through the fat on the pork in parallel lines about 1cm/½ inch apart. You don't want to go completely through to the flesh but make sure they are good crevasses that can be pulled apart fairly easily when you come to rub salt into them.

3 Place the five spice, red chilli flakes, pepper, 1 tablespoon salt, sugar and garlic in a bowl and add 2 tablespoons of the oil. Mix well and then rub onto the bottom of the pork belly (onto the flesh). Then flip over and rub about 1 tablespoon sea salt into the fat on top of the belly and finish by pouring over the remaining tablespoon of oil.

4 Place the joint into a roasting tray. Roast in the hot oven for 30 minutes until the fat becomes crisp and puffy. Turn the heat down to 160°C/325°F/Gas Mark 3 and cook for a further 2 hours. This slow cooking will leave you with wonderfully tender meat yet a crispy top.

5 Remove the meat from the oven and leave to rest on a board for 10 minutes while you put together your accompaniments. Carve slices vertically and tear off the ribs, I tend to put all the slices and ribs on a big board and let everyone dive in. Sensational.

❖**TIFF'S TIPS** I'd serve this one of two ways: traditionally with crispy small potatoes and a selection of tasty vegetables, or with steaming buttered rice, some coriander and a stir-fry of oriental vegetables. Try pak choi, green beans and sugar snap peas doused with soy and lime juice and eat it out of the bowl all together – great soul food.

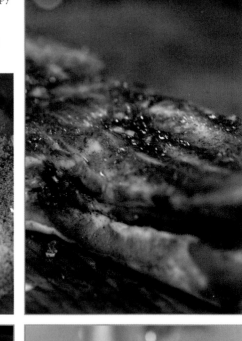

❖**LEFTOVERS** There's often some delicious leftover pork after a big roast. Try to resist grazing on leftovers as you potter round the kitchen and keep the pork for a lovely pork and apple sandwich, or for a pork stir-fry. Just throw together all your weekend leftovers on a Sunday or Monday night. I also love a creamy pork pasta sauce. Shred the leftover meat and mix it with a carbonara type sauce and tagliatelle for a lovely leftover feast.

❖**TIFF'S TIPS** A miniature version can be served on cocktail sticks as party nibbles. Make them in the morning, keep them covered in the fridge along with the dip, and then cook them at the last minute.

❖**LEFTOVERS** A really interesting and delicious leftover idea is to serve them inside a sweet potato. Sounds random but so fun. Alternatively, you could remove them from the skewers and serve them as meatballs with the traditional spaghetti and slow cooked tomato sauce.

SHOPPING LIST

Koftas:
500g/1lb 2oz lean minced lamb
1 red onion, chopped finely
3 garlic cloves
2 tablespoons ground cumin
1 pinch of chilli flakes
3 tablespoons coriander, chopped
2 tablespoons lemon juice
1 small egg
salt and freshly ground
    black pepper

Dip:
150ml/5fl oz plain yoghurt
3 tablespoons mint, chopped
2 tablespoons lemon juice
1 teaspoon cumin
1 teaspoon red cayenne pepper

4 wooden skewers, soaked in
water to avoid burning

TIFF'S LAMB KOFTA GRECIAN KEBABS ✪✪ SERVES 4

"I love Greece and these are inspired by a popular Greek dish – gorgeous morsels of juicy lamb on skewers served with a tsatsiki dip. Lamb mince is reasonably priced and easy to spice up with lots of gorgeous earthy flavours – cumin works particularly well."

1 Mix all the kofta ingredients together in a bowl and season well.

2 Divide the mixture into 12 medium size balls and shape them into little oval koftas.

3 Thread three koftas onto each of the pre-soaked skewers. Once they are all done, keep them in the fridge while you make the dip.

4 Place all the dip ingredients in a bowl and mix together.

5 Heat a griddle pan over a high heat and add a few of the lamb koftas, cooking them for 3–4 minutes on each side until brown.

6 Allow the meat to rest for 2–3 minutes before serving with the bowl of dip. A selection of grilled vegetables and couscous work brilliantly on the side, as does a big salad with pine nuts, feta cheese and cucumber.

SHOPPING LIST

500g/1lb 2oz lamb mince
1 teaspoon cumin
1 teaspoon ground coriander
½ red onion, chopped finely
2 garlic cloves, crushed
2 tablespoons rosemary,
   chopped finely
2 sprigs mint, chopped
1 teaspoon lemon juice

5 tablespoons olive oil
125g/4½oz halloumi cheese, cut
   into slices
4 ciabatta rolls, opened
rocket leaves, to serve
salt and freshly ground black
   pepper

Tsatsiki:

6 tablespoons plain yoghurt
2 tablespoons crème fraîche
½ cucumber, chopped finely
½ teaspoon cumin
1 garlic clove, peeled and crushed
2 teaspoons olive oil
2 teaspoons lemon juice

EPIC GREEK
LAMB BURGER ✪✪ MAKES 4

❝My boyfriend and I were inspired by these on a trip to a London food market – they were heaving with cumin and zingy mint. I recreated them at home and came up with this recipe. With the herbs, fresh tsatsiki and the hot halloumi to finish it's brilliant for an easy yet innovative weeknight supper.❞

1 In a large bowl mix together the lamb mince, cumin, coriander, red onion, garlic, rosemary, mint and lemon juice. Season with salt and pepper and bind the mixture together with 2 tablespoons of the olive oil.

2 Shape the lamb mixture into four burgers and put them in the fridge for 5–10 minutes to firm up.

3 Meanwhile make the tsatsiki. Mix the yoghurt, crème fraîche, cucumber, cumin, garlic, olive oil and lemon juice. Season and set aside.

4 Heat the remaining oil in a frying pan over a medium heat then add the burgers. Cook for 4–5 minutes on each side.

5 Gently fry the halloumi slices for 2 minutes on each side until they are golden brown.

6 Now place the ciabatta rolls on a dry pan, under the grill or in a grill pan to toast for a couple of minutes on each side.

7 Assemble your burgers. Place the rocket leaves on one half of the toasted rolls, drizzle with olive oil and sprinkle with sea salt.

8 Bung on the burger and top with delicious tsatsiki and a slice of halloumi. Put the top bun op top. Serve with a big green salad, absolutely delish!

❖**TIFF'S TIPS** When pan frying the burgers don't try and turn them too much, as they are quite delicate until the sugars in the meat caramelise and give the burger a crust below. Then you can turn them after about 4 minutes.

❖**OPTIONAL EXTRAS** Swap the beef for pork or chicken mince and add the flavourings you would like. With chicken I like to add sundried tomatoes and lots of cheese, and serve with a fresh mayonnaise. Pork burgers are brilliant with fresh apple sauce.

4

HOT
DATES

When you've got a date coming over for
dinner, you'll want to impress without
being stuck in the kitchen all night.
Flavoured butter melting on a juicy steak is
simple, yet oh so delicious. Or dive in and
share a bowl of garlicy moules marinières.

HOW TO MAKE
GARLIC AND PARSLEY BUTTER ✲

SHOPPING LIST
100g/3½oz butter, softened
2–3 garlic cloves, crushed
3 tablespoons finely chopped
   parsley
salt and freshly ground black
   pepper

Flavoured butters can transform a simple piece of fish or meat. Whip a few slices out of the fridge and serve on grilled or barbecued meat for instant va-va-voom.

1 Remove the butter from the fridge a good hour or so before making this and place it in a bowl. Use a wooden spoon to cream it until it's lovely and soft. Add the herbs and season well.

2 Tip the butter onto a piece of cling film. Then roll it up into a sausage shape, tie the ends so it looks like a Christmas cracker and place in the fridge to harden.

3 When it comes to serving, just slice 2½cm/1inch of the butter per person.

ROSEMARY AND SAGE BUTTER ✲

SHOPPING LIST
100g/3½oz butter, softened
2 tablespoons chopped sage leaves
3 sprigs of rosemary, chopped
   finely
½ teaspoon lemon juice
salt and freshly ground black
   pepper

This butter is particularly good with roasted root vegetables and is also wonderful to melt over a lovely lamb chop.

1 Remove the butter from the fridge a good hour or so before making this and place it in a bowl. Use a wooden spoon to cream it until it's lovely and soft. Add the herbs and lemon juice and season well.

2 Place a piece of cling film on your work surface and tip the butter onto it. Then roll it up into a sausage shape, tie the ends and place in the fridge to harden.

3 When it comes to serving, just slice 2½cm/1inch of the butter per person.

CHILLI BUTTER ✲

SHOPPING LIST
100g/3½oz butter, softened
½ teaspoon chilli flakes
½ teaspoon lemon juice
salt and freshly ground black
   pepper

Brilliant with fish, and wonderful to melt over linguine. It's also fantastic melted into a risotto and great to give a stir-fry extra punch.

1 Remove the butter from the fridge a good hour or so before making this and place it in a bowl. Use a wooden spoon to cream it until it's lovely and soft.

2 Now add the chilli flakes and the lemon juice. Season well with salt and pepper.

3 Place a piece of cling film on your work surface and tip the butter onto it. Then roll it up into a sausage shape, tie the ends and place in the fridge to harden.

4 When it comes to serving, just slice 2½cm/1inch of the butter per person.

2 egg yolks
½ teaspoon English or Dijon
   mustard
1 tablespoon white wine vinegar
200ml/7fl oz vegetable oil
80ml/2½fl oz olive oil
1 lemon, quartered, plus 2 slices
   to garnish
2–3 tablespoons ketchup

½ iceberg lettuce, shredded
2 celery sticks, finely chopped
150g/5½oz small cooked
   peeled prawns
1 small ripe avocado
pinch of cayenne pepper
salt and freshly ground black
   pepper

RETURN OF RETRO – AVOCADO AND PRAWN COCKTAIL SERVES 2 ✪ ✪ ✪

"I think the key to a really good prawn cocktail is fresh mayonnaise, which tastes a million times better than ready-made. Forget the notion of it being tricky. If you take your time and follow the steps it won't go wrong. The main thing to remember is to add the oil *slowly* or it will split as it hits your egg and vinegar combo."

1 Whisk together the egg yolks, mustard and wine vinegar until well combined. Season lightly.

2 Mix the two oils together in a jug. Now with your whisk in one hand the whole time and the oil in the other, very slowly add the oil bit by bit to the egg mixture, whisking all the time. Let it trickle really slowly – if you pour too much at once it will split.

3 The more oil you add the thicker the mayonnaise will become. When all the oil is incorporated, taste and adjust the seasoning.

4 Now add the juice from one of the lemon quarters, followed by the ketchup. This is your Marie Rose sauce.

5 Place the shredded lettuce in a small mixing bowl and add the celery. Take a tablespoon, spoon on 2–3 tablespoons of your sauce and toss well. You don't want it to be too saucy, as that will overpower all those other flavours, but it should be lightly coated.

6 Spoon the lettuce mix into shallow glasses or bowls, filling them fairly high.

7 Place the prawns on top. Cut the avocado in half and remove the stone. Now peel away the skin from both halves and using a sharp knife cut the avocado into thin slices. Arrange the avocado on top of the prawns and garnish with a small slice of lemon. Add a pinch of cayenne pepper, if you like.

❖LEFTOVERS If you have leftover mayonnaise, keep it in the fridge and serve it with crudités, on toast with a gorgeous topping, or combined with some crushed garlic and served with a lovely crisp chicken breast and salad for a simple supper.

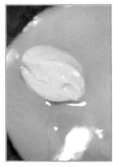

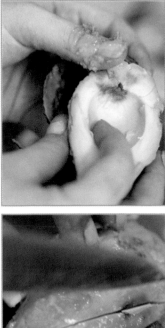

❖OPTIONAL EXTRAS You can pay as much or as little as you like for the ingredients in a prawn cocktail: you could serve thrifty precooked and shelled prawns, or tiger prawns, or go all out with lobster collops.

SHOPPING LIST
2 large chicken breasts
150g/5½oz garlic and parsley butter (see pages 76–7)
4–6 slices of Parma ham (optional)
100g/3½oz plain flour
2 eggs, beaten
150g/5½oz breadcrumbs
2–3 tablespoons olive oil

CHICKEN KIEV WITH GARLIC AND PARSLEY BUTTER SERVES 2 ❷

"There is something impressive and satisfying about making a fresh chicken kiev. My sister is a hoover when it comes to them – we used to have chicken kiev as a staple Friday night supper as children. The Parma ham makes it by adding an extra salty flavour.

You can prepare these kievs the morning before you cook them, so you're not faffing in the kitchen at the last minute."

1 Preheat the oven to 200°C/400°F/Gas Mark 6.

2 Take the chicken breasts and carefully remove the mini fillet, which will be only partially attached anyway. Make a careful slit lengthways through the fillet, taking care not to cut right through to the other side of the breast.

3 Stuff half the garlic butter mixture in the little pocket and fold the chicken back across the slit.

4 Now, I use Parma ham in my kievs, first for the flavour and second because it seems to help keep all the juices firmly in the kiev. You can, however, just skip this step if you prefer. Place 2–3 slices of Parma ham on a piece of cling film and then lay the stuffed chicken breast on one edge of the Parma ham layers. Roll the Parma ham around the chicken, using the cling film to guide you until it's tightly wrapped.

5 Wrap in cling film and chill in the fridge for 30 minutes to firm up.

6 Put the flour, beaten egg and breadcrumbs into three separate bowls. Take the kievs and dunk them each first in the flour, coating well, then into the egg and last in the breadcrumbs. They should be equally covered.

7 Heat a pan with the oil and fry for 3–4 minutes on each side. Transfer to an ovenproof dish and finish cooking in the oven for about 15 minutes.

8 Remove from the oven – they should be golden brown and firm to touch. Serve immediately and when you cut open the juice will pop and run out. Garlic butter heaven, and if you're on a date it won't matter because you're both eating it.

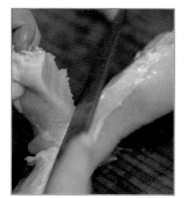

❖**TIFF'S TIPS** Make sure the butter is really cold when you add it to the chicken. You need to keep it entirely in the chicken so the juices don't run out all over the place.

❖**OPTIONAL EXTRAS** I love to serve this with rice, mash or a little spaghetti.

SHOPPING LIST

600g/1lb 5oz mussels
25g/1oz butter
3 garlic cloves, peeled and crushed
1 small onion, finely chopped
70ml/2½fl oz dry white wine
60ml/2fl oz double cream
large handful parsley, chopped coarsely
salt and freshly ground black pepper
French bread, to serve

MOULES MARINIÈRES SERVES 2 ✪ ✪

" This is a classic French dish and seen all over brasserie menus; however, it's one of the easiest and, perhaps surprisingly, cheapest meals due to the low price of mussels. They are abundant on exposed shores and so are a thrifty choice. "

1 Place the mussels in a colander and rinse them thoroughly. Discard any mussels that remain open. Remove any residue from the shells, which sometimes resembles beards. Give them a good scrub if needed.

2 Melt the butter in a large deep saucepan, then add the garlic and onion and soften gently over a low heat for 3–4 minutes.

3 Tip in the mussels and stir really well. Season well and coat them in all the delicious flavours.

4 Add the white wine and place the lid on your pan. This creates a steaming effect.

5 After about 4 minutes you'll notice the mussels (or majority of them) have opened. Discard any that remain closed. Now you can add the cream and parsley.

6 Warm for a further minute, taste and season. The sauce should be gloriously garlicky and rich.

7 Serve in deep bowls with some crusty French bread.

❖**TIFF'S TIPS** Mussels, like all seafood and shellfish, must be fresh. Never eat them if they remain closed after cooking. This is true of clams as well. During the cooking process, the shells of the mussels will open right up when they are ready to be eaten.

❖**TIFF'S TIPS** Clams aren't as economical as mussels, but I adore them with a simple wine and garlic sauce. This is achieved by gently frying some slightly bruised garlic cloves in a lot of butter and then adding some white wine and the clams along with lots of coriander. Gorgeous and very simple, so worth a try.

❖**TIFF'S TIPS** This recipe is also great as party nibbles. Serve instead in baby gem lettuce leaves – perfect with drinks.

❖**LEFTOVERS** For a very special lunch, spoon any leftover stir-fry into a wrap along with some shredded lettuce, cucumber strips and a drizzle of hoi-sin sauce.

SHOPPING LIST

2 tablespoons sunflower oil

250g/9oz pork mince

2 garlic cloves, peeled and
  crushed

2cm/1inch piece ginger, peeled
  and sliced finely

1 teaspoon chilli flakes

1 spring onion, chopped

4 mushrooms, chopped finely

2 tablespoons soy sauce

1 teaspoon honey

1 teaspoon Chinese five spice

juice of 1 lime

2–3 tablespoons hoi-sin sauce

large handful coriander, finely
  chopped

iceberg lettuce, separated into
  individual leaves

STICKY PORK STIR-FRY LETTUCE CUPS ✪✪ SERVES 2

"This is my version of the lettuce cups you get with gooey pork or duck at Chinese restaurants. I make this with pork mince, which is tasty and economical. For a more extravagant dish try using small pieces of stir-fried duck. It's irresistible finger food – delicious and a great ice breaker!"

1 Heat about 1 tablespoon of oil in a wok or frying pan then add the pork mince and fry for 3–4 minutes. Remove from the pan and set aside. Wipe the wok, as you will use it again.

2 Heat the wok again with another tablespoon of oil. When hot add the garlic, ginger strips, chilli flakes and spring onion. Stir fry for a couple of minutes until you start to smell all their amazing flavours.

3 Add the mushrooms and the cooked pork mince followed by the soy sauce, honey, Chinese five spice and lime juice. Fry for about 1 minute, taste and season. Taste and add more soy sauce or lime juice if needed.

4 Spoon into the lettuce leaves, place on a big serving dish and drizzle the hoi-sin sauce over each one. Top with chopped coriander and serve.

❖**TIFF'S TIPS** There's a prawn for every budget: buy small precooked shelled prawns for economical value, or use raw tiger prawns if you're splashing out. This dish is also magnificent with clams, making the Italian classic Spaghetti alle Vongole.

❖**LEFTOVERS** Use any leftover sauce as a delicious topping for bruschetta or crostini.

SHOPPING LIST

250g/9oz linguine
2 tablespoons olive oil
2 garlic cloves, crushed and
    chopped finely
1 red onion, chopped finely
1 large red chilli, deseeded and
    sliced
2 large tomatoes, chopped

zest and juice of ½ lemon
1 glass of white wine
500g/1lb 2oz peeled raw prawns
handful chopped flat-leaf
    parsley
lemon wedges, to serve
salt and freshly ground
    black pepper

PUNCHY PRAWNS WITH CHILLI, TOMATO AND OLIVE OIL LINGUINE
SERVES 2 ✪ ✪

"This is so gorgeous, a great dish to impress, yet simple to make. I think this is one of my favourites for a hot date or just when someone special comes round. Who needs lip-plumping lipstick when you have chillies? It's hot, tangy and big on flavour. Feel free to substitute the prawns with crab, clams or mussels, they all work well. Light some candles, dim the lights and you're off. "

1 Slide the linguine into a saucepan of boiling water, add a splash of olive oil and a pinch of salt and cook for 8–10 minutes until al dente.

2 Meanwhile heat 1 tablespoon of oil in a large saucepan. Add the garlic, onion, chilli and tomatoes and cook over a medium heat until soft. Season well with salt and pepper.

3 Add the lemon juice and zest, and the white wine. Taste and adjust the seasoning.

4 Thrown in the prawns, and cook for 3–4 minutes until they turn from grey to pink.

5 Drain the linguine and add it to the chilli white wine sauce. Mix well, season with lots of black pepper and add the parsley.

6 Drizzle with the remaining olive oil and serve with lemon wedges.

SHOPPING LIST

2 rump steaks
1 tablespoons olive oil
4 large potatoes, such as
  Maris Piper
2–3 tablespoons sunflower
  or vegetable oil
2 large tomatoes, halved

1 quantity of flavoured butter,
  such as chilli or garlic and
  parsley (see pages 76–7)
salad leaves, to serve
sea salt and freshly ground black
  pepper

SEARED STEAK WITH RUSTIC CHIPS AND CHILLI BUTTER SERVES 2 ✪✪✪

"I cannot stress enough the importance of good quality meat. Visit your butcher, tell him your budget and don't be nervous if you are unsure which cut to get. He is there to help you. Rump steak is very delicious and a thrifty cut. The rump of the cow is literally the entire back end, and there is a lot of it, hence the low price! However, if your budget allows, branch out and buy sirloin, rib eye or fillet. "

1 Preheat the oven to 200°C/400°F/Gas Mark 6.

2 Place the steaks on a plate, rub with the olive oil and lots of sea salt and pepper and leave to rest. It's always crucial to leave meat to return to room temperature before cooking it, as you need to allow the muscles to relax and thus absorb all the flavours.

3 Take your potatoes – I like the skin left on, but it's up to you – and cut them into thick chips.

4 Meanwhile pour the sunflower or vegetable oil into a baking tray and place in the oven to heat up for 3–4 minutes.

5 Carefully slip your chips into the tray of hot oil, scatter with lots of sea salt to get them super crispy and put them in the oven.

6 Cook for 30–35 minutes until crispy and golden but soft inside. After 15 minutes place the 4 tomato halves on the same tray and spoon a bit of the oil over them. The tomatoes are done when they are soft and slightly charring.

7 About 5 minutes before the chips are done, heat a frying pan or a grill pan with no oil and when it's smoking place the steaks on the hot pan. For rare cook for 1½–2 minutes on each side, for medium 2–3 minutes on each side and for well done 4–5 minutes on each side. Remove from the pan and leave to rest for 5 minutes.

8 Serve with a slice of flavoured butter – the heat of the steak will melt it deliciously. Accompany with the chips, tomatoes and a handful of salad leaves.

❖**LEFTOVERS** I doubt even after a hot date you will have any leftovers, as it's far too succulent and delish not to finish, but if there are, keep the leftover beef for a delicious cold steak sandwich with mustard and rocket the next day.

SHOPPING LIST

2 duck breasts, skin on
2–3 tablespoons soy sauce
2 tablespoons honey
2 red chillies, sliced
4 tablespoons vegetable oil
2 spring onions, chopped
2 pak choi, leaves separated
1 tablespoon soy sauce
juice of 1 lime

STICKY ORIENTAL DUCK BREASTS WITH PAK CHOI

SERVES 2 ✪✪✪

" I have been told by friends that this is the best way I cook duck. With the flesh marinated with the fabulous and successful marriage of soy and honey and the skin scored and plumped with lashings of sea salt to achieve the ultimate crispy skin, this is a winner. Duck is a huge treat and perfect for a winter date. "

1 Preheat the oven to 200°C/400°F/Gas Mark 6.

2 Take the duck breasts and score the skin not quite through to the meat. Rub with about 1 teaspoon sea salt for each duck breast (don't panic, the majority falls off, but this will make the skin super crispy and crackly).

3 Place the duck breasts in a dish, pour over the soy sauce and honey, and sprinkle with half the red chillies. If you have time, leave to marinate for anything from 30 minutes to 2 hours, but even just few minutes is better than nothing.

4 Take a non-stick pan and heat 2–3 tablespoons of the vegetable oil. When sizzling add the duck breasts skin side down for 3 minutes, then turn over and cook for 4–5 minutes. Keep a firm eye on the pan, as the honey can burn quite quickly.

5 Tip it all into an ovenproof dish and transfer to the oven for 8–10 minutes.

6 Meanwhile heat the remaining tablespoon of oil in a wok or large frying pan. When hot add the remaining chopped red chilli, the spring onions and then the pak choi. Fry for a couple of minutes and then add the soy sauce and lime juice.

7 Remove the duck breasts from the oven and leave them to rest for a few minutes.

8 Slice the duck breasts diagonally and serve with the stir-fried vegetables. Spoon over the sauce and tuck in.

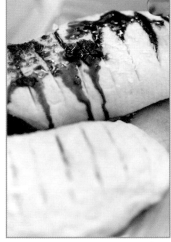

❖LEFTOVERS If you find yourself with leftover slices of duck, use them for a supper-for-one duck curry. Simply fry some ginger and chilli, then add a little red curry paste, some coconut milk, coriander and your duck pieces. Serve with some rice.

5

WEEKEND BRUNCH

I love a lazy Saturday with the papers and a feast. Eggs Benedict is just the ticket for two, and when you're feeding the troops Easy Peasy American Pancakes will sort out any heavy heads. If you're feeling virtuous, fresh fruit salad is the way to start your day, or you could feast like a king and go for the full Champion's Breakfast fry-up.

HOW TO MAKE
EASY HOLLANDAISE SAUCE ✪✪✪ MAKES 250ML/9FL OZ

SHOPPING LIST
3 egg yolks
½ teaspoon Dijon or
    English mustard
1 tablespoon lemon juice
175g/6oz butter
salt and freshly ground black
    pepper

This is one of the emulsion sauces and is related to mayonnaise and béarnaise. It's my favourite, as it's a crucial part of one of my favourite dishes of all time, Eggs Benedict (see pages 96–7). Hollandaise sauce goes with anything and everything from brunch dishes to asparagus. It's very much thought of as a decadent treat, which probably stems from the belief that it's a challenge to make with its reputation of curdling quickly. Fear no more! Armed with this recipe, and by keeping your wits about you, your efforts will be a tremendous success. It's a recipe that you will use time and time again. You can use the same recipe and method if you fancy using a blender.

1 Place the egg yolks (keep the whites for meringues or freeze them), mustard, lemon juice and salt and pepper in a bowl and mix well.

2 Melt the butter in a saucepan until foaming.

3 Very carefully pour the butter bit by tiny bit onto the egg mixture, whisking all the time. Start very, very gradually and after a while you will notice it thicken.

4 The finished sauce should be thick enough to coat the back of a spoon. Taste it and adjust the seasoning if needed. Keep at room temperature.

❖TIFF'S TIPS For a super speedy cheat's béarnaise sauce, simply add about 2 tablespoons chopped tarragon to your hollandaise. Serve with a juicy steak.

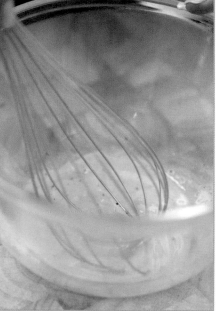

❖LEFTOVERS Hollandaise goes with so much, not just poached eggs. I love it poured generously on top of fishcakes and served with a simple salad. It's also lovely with steamed asparagus as a treat in the warmer months.

EGGS BENEDICT SERVES 1 ✪✪✪

SHOPPING LIST
1 tablespoon vegetable or
    sunflower oil
2 rashers bacon
1 English muffin, halved
2 eggs
1 teaspoon butter
4–5 tablespoons Hollandaise
    Sauce (see pages 94–5)

Eggs Benedict is on every restaurant or café brunch menu but is so achievable within your own home. Traditionally it's made with ham, but I always serve it with crispy bacon and for me there is no going back; but do replace with slices of ham if you prefer.

1 Take a frying pan and heat the oil and then fry the bacon for 5 minutes. Whilst you're doing this you could make your hollandaise sauce.

2 Remove the bacon from the pan and place it on kitchen paper to drain.

3 Clean the frying pan, then pour 3½cm/1/½inch boiling water into it. Meanwhile place the muffin halves in the toaster.

4 Bring the water back up to the boil then break the eggs into it. Cook on high for about 20 seconds then reduce the heat to low-medium and poach for a further 3–4 minutes.

5 Butter the muffins and place a rasher of bacon on each half. Using a slotted spoon remove both eggs and place one on each muffin half.

6 Now spoon over 2 tablespoons of hollandaise per poached egg and don't wait for anything, just eat!

EGGS FLORENTINE SERVES 1 ✪✪✪

SHOPPING LIST
1 tablespoon olive oil
handful spinach
2 eggs
1 English muffin, halved
1 teaspoon butter
4–5 tablespoons Hollandaise
    Sauce (see pages 94–5)

This is the vegetarian option for Eggs Benedict and still absolutely delicious. It's also a fantastic way to use up spinach. Occasionally I use rocket instead of spinach, which is fantastic as well.

1 Heat the oil in a pan and when hot add the spinach. Just flash in the pan for a minute, then remove to a plate and set aside.

2 Clean the frying pan, then pour 3½cm/1/½inches boiling water into it. Meanwhile place the muffin halves in the toaster.

3 Bring the water back up to the boil then break the eggs into it. Cook on high for about 20 seconds, then reduce the heat to low-medium and poach for a further 3–4 minutes.

4 Butter the muffin and divide the spinach between the two halves. Using a slotted spoon remove both eggs and place them on top of the spinach.

5 Spoon over 2 tablespoons of hollandaise per poached egg and serve.

SHOPPING LIST
1 tablespoon sunflower oil
2 rashers streaky bacon
100g/3½oz chorizo, chopped finely
1 teaspoon lemon juice
2 eggs
6 chives, snipped

BAKED EGGS – ¡OLÉ! SERVES 2 ✪✪

❝ Baked eggs, simply cooked on their own in ramekins, have a very simple clean taste – like a healthy pure fried egg. They can, however, also make good supporting acts for bigger flavours. Chorizo adds a good blast of spice and herbs work well, as they give a subtle shadow of flavour. For a big brunch dish, place lots of eggs in an ovenproof dish, season and dive in with buttered soldiers. ❞

1 Preheat the oven to 180°C/350°F/Gas Mark 4.

2 Heat the oil in a frying pan and when hot add the bacon and chorizo. Cook for a few minutes until crispy. Add the lemon juice.

3 Take two ramekins or very small ovenproof dishes (alternatively you could cook both eggs in one dish) and spoon in the delicious lemony chorizo and bacon. Crack the eggs on top and put them in the oven.

4 Cook for 10–12 minutes until set. Then serve sprinkled with snipped chives.

❖**TIFF'S TIPS** Be really careful about not allowing the eggs to overcook, as this will make your yolk a really pale yellow and all shrivelled up like a prune. Keep a steely eye on them...

❖**OPTIONAL EXTRAS** I love to eat this with hot buttered toast to scoop out all the delicious flavours along with the dripping butter – glorious.

150ml/5fl oz water
1 teaspoon sugar
3 ripe plums, halved and stone
  removed
4 tablespoons yoghurt
2 tablespoons honey

POACHED PLUMS WITH YOGHURT AND HONEY ✪ SERVES 2

"Well worth a little effort for a special breakfast, this is not only healthy but also deliciously filling. With a little forward planning, you can poach the fruit and leave it in the fridge in its juices for the week and just tuck in for a quick breakfast, take it to work or even have it as a midweek healthy pudding. I've used plums here, but you can use whatever fruit is in season."

1 Bring the water and sugar to the boil. Slide in the plum halves and simmer until they are soft, about 8–10 minutes.

2 When done, remove the plums from the pan and set them cut-side up in two bowls, spooning over the sugary juices.

3 Top each bowlful with a couple of tablespoons of yoghurt and finish with a good drizzle of honey.

❖**OPTIONAL EXTRAS** In the heat of summer I use this method to poach strawberries and raspberries but they don't need as long as the plums, so just poach them for 3–4 minutes. Pears are also delicious, and you can poach them in the same way and serve with melted chocolate for a very retro classic pud.

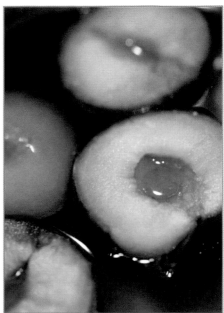

❖**TIFF'S TIPS** This authentic British dish is traditionally served with chips dunked into the creamy rich yolk, so feel free to serve some tiny crispy frites on the side. Always remember to season your eggs well. Salt transforms them!

SHOPPING LIST

1 tablespoon sunflower or vegetable oil
4 large slices good quality thick ham or
　　gammon, smoked or unsmoked
4 eggs
2 breakfast muffins
2 tablespoons butter
salt and freshly ground black pepper

TRADITIONAL HAM 'N' EGGS

SERVES 2 ✪✪

❝This is a refined way of serving Ham 'n' Eggs, rather than the greasy version found in too many cafés. Nevertheless, crispy frites still work beautifully on the side. Springtime spinach folded through the layers would be a delicious addition.❞

1 Take a good frying pan and heat the oil.

2 When hot, add the slices of good thick ham and just bronze for a minute or two on each side. Take out of the pan and leave to drain on some kitchen towel.

3 Now crack the eggs into the pan to fry for 2–3 minutes. You want a gorgeous soft yolk, so do this on a low heat.

4 Meanwhile toast your muffins and then butter them.

5 Place the bottom muffin on a plate and begin to assemble. I like to layer the ham and eggs. Don't forget to season the layers. Just pop your top muffin on top of your breakfast tower and repeat with the second muffin!

6 How you tackle it is up to you: knife and fork of course is good but I tend to grab a napkin and take a big bite.

❖**TIFF'S TIPS** Serve with streaky bacon and honey or golden syrup – stack them high, tucking a bacon rasher in between each layer and then drizzle over the syrup or honey.

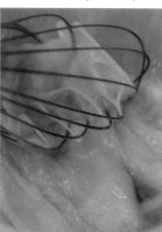

❖**LEFTOVERS** Serve leftover pancakes at teatime with jam and butter, or have them warm with vanilla ice cream as a delicious dessert.

6 tablespoons butter
280g/10oz self-raising flour
1 teaspoon salt
4 tablespoons caster sugar
2 eggs, beaten
250ml/9fl oz milk
6–8 rashers of bacon
1 teaspoon vegetable oil
golden syrup, to serve

EASY PEASY AMERICAN PANCAKES ✪✪

MAKES 8–10 PANCAKES

❝This recipe makes about 8–10 pancakes. I like to have them in the fridge over the weekend for if friends pop in for brekkie, which they always do. The pancakes can be kept in an airtight bag in the fridge for up to 3 days. They can be reheated either in a pan or in the microwave.❞

1 Preheat the oven to 150°C/300°F/Gas Mark 2.

2 Heat 5 tablespoons of the butter in a saucepan over a medium heat, then set aside.

3 Sieve the flour into a large bowl. Add the salt and sugar.

4 Add the melted butter to the beaten eggs, then make a well in the flour mixture and add the milk, and the egg and butter mixture, whisking with a hand whisk to beat through any lumps.

5 Heat the remaining tablespoon of butter in a frying pan, then add a ladleful of batter. It should be about 1cm/½ inch thick. Cook for 1–2 minutes on each side until golden brown. Keep the pancakes warm on a plate in the oven while you cook the rest of the batch.

6 Meanwhile fry the bacon in the oil until crispy, then layer between the pancakes. Drizzle with golden syrup and serve.

SHOPPING LIST

1 pineapple, peeled and cut into
   chunks
1 Galia or Cantaloupe melon,
   halved, deseeded and cubed
3 oranges, peeled and cut into
   chunks
2 mangoes (summer), cut into
   chunks
2 pomegranates (winter), halved
   and seeds removed

2 pears (winter), peeled,
   deseeded and cut into chunks
handful of berries, blackberries,
   blueberries, raspberries,
   strawberries, cranberries
   (depending on season)
1 glass of orange juice
1 teaspoon lemon juice

SEASONAL FRUIT SALAD ✪ SERVES 2

"Every brunch needs a good fruit salad on the side. Make the most of seasonal fruit by throwing them together and covering them in orange juice for a refreshing fruit salad. In winter you can choose from pomegranates, pears, blackberries, passion fruit and clementines while summer brings delicious mangoes, raspberries and strawberries."

1 Place all the fruit you are using in a large bowl and mix well.

2 Pour over the orange juice and lemon juice and mix well.

❖**TIFF'S TIPS** If you find yourself with guests and time does not allow you to make a pudding, throw a fruit salad together. Serve in small tumblers for a nicely presented touch and, if you are celebrating, you could even add a little prosecco.

❖**OPTIONAL EXTRAS** I love to sprinkle over a good handful of muesli or oats, as this blends in beautifully. Serve with some plain yoghurt too, if you like.

❖**LEFTOVERS** If you're cooking for a few more people I always find there are leftover bits of bacon and sausages. Don't throw them away, as bacon can be cut up into a pasta dish such as the amatriciana penne pasta bake (see page 44–5), and mushrooms can go into an omelette.

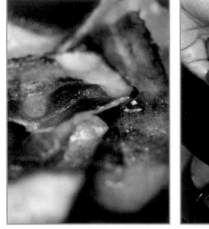

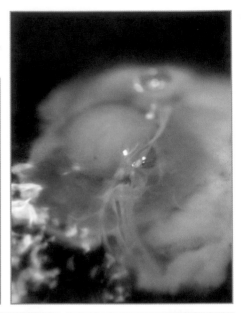

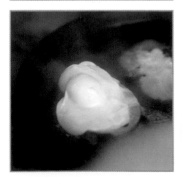

❖**TIFF'S TIPS** Don't panic if it looks like it's all going to be ready before the eggs are done – it can all be kept warm for up to half an hour in a 110°C/225F/Gas Mark ¼ oven. Cover loosely with foil if you like. Get yourself completely ready before you cook the eggs.

SHOPPING LIST

2 tablespoons sunflower oil
4 rashers unsmoked streaky bacon
100g/3½oz mushrooms, sliced
8 cherry tomatoes, halved
2 muffins
2 eggs
2 tablespoons butter
salt and freshly ground black pepper

THE CHAMPION'S BREAKFAST SERVES 2 ✪✪✪

"I cook this for my man before he plays footie on Saturday mornings. One morning he ate it and proceeded to score four amazing goals – he came back and told me it was all because of breakfast, which was subsequently coined 'The Champion's Breakfast'. So if you need a bit of weekend oomph, then this is for you. There is definitely an art to poached eggs, but I love them so much I feel confident to say that I have perfected the art."

1 Preheat the oven to 150°C/300°F/Gas Mark 2.

2 Heat the oil in a frying pan then fry the bacon for 3–4 minutes on each side until crispy and golden. Place on an ovenproof dish in the warm oven.

3 Using the same frying pan, fry the mushrooms for 4–5 minutes until cooked and slightly crispy, if the pan is too dry, add a tablespoon of butter to loosen it all up. After about 2 minutes add the cherry tomatoes to the pan and season well. Give them another 3 minutes, then tip into the ovenproof dish in the oven.

4 Clean the frying pan and pour in 3½cm/1/1½in boiling water.

5 Toast the muffins and then break your eggs into the boiling water in the frying pan. Keep on high for about 20 seconds and then turn down to low-medium and cook gently for a further 3–4 minutes. Then turn off the heat.

6 Butter the muffins and divide the bacon, mushrooms and cherry tomatoes between the two slices. Using a slotted spoon, remove both eggs and serve with lots of black pepper and salt. Then grab your tea, the paper and put your weekend feet up!

6

FOOD
TO SHARE

Whatever the occasion this chapter
has food perfect for entertaining.
Bring a serving dish to the table and
let everyone help themselves. Take
your time with the cooking and make
a special effort. What better way to
impress friends and family?

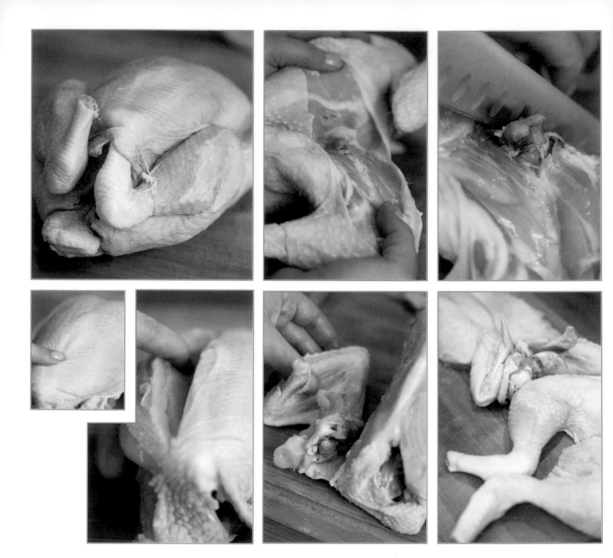

❖**TIFF'S TIPS** When you're using stock from the fridge reheat it to boiling point first. With frozen stock, defrost it completely and then heat till boiling.

HOW TO JOINT A CHICKEN ✪✪✪

SHOPPING LIST

1 large free-range chicken
1 strong knife
1 board

Jointing a chicken is a savvy way to use one bird to dish up a number of different and delicious meals throughout your week. It's great for your budget, as just one chicken can make not only a sensual stock, and spicy crispy chicken wings, but also stuffed chicken breasts and coq au vin.

1 Place the chicken on the chopping board with the legs towards you and the breast away from you.

2 Take a knife and, starting with the right leg, gently slide it through the skin, pulling the leg away from the carcass at the same time. This will reveal the knuckle socket holding the leg to the body. Cut through the ball and socket. Use your hands to help you by pulling it as well. Let your knife guide you. Now you have removed the leg and thigh.

3 Do this with the other leg too.

4 Now run your finger along the breastbone, either side of which are the two breasts. Take your knife slightly at an angle and run it down the carcass, freeing the first breast. Do the same with the other side.

5 See the wings sticking out? Take a knife and simply cut through the ball and socket of each wing. Voilà! One jointed chicken, ready to cook.

FRESH CHICKEN STOCK ✪ MAKES 1.2 LITRES/42FL OZ

SHOPPING LIST

1 large free-range chicken carcass,
    meat removed
1 large onion
3–4 carrots, roughly chopped
any leftover raw vegetables, such
    as parsnips, celery or leek
handful black peppercorns
1.5 litres/52fl oz water

I am very aware as a foodie that there are good stock cubes on the market now, some of which are even endorsed by chefs. Nevertheless, for me homemade stock remains a class apart. It's packed with flavour and fills the house with a wonderful smell as you make it. It takes 5 minutes at most to bung everything into the saucepan and then you can put your feet up and let it simmer away. It couldn't be simpler, and after investing in a delicious chicken it seems almost deplorable to discard the empty carcass.

1 Place all ingredients into a big saucepan and set on a low-medium heat to simmer for about 3 hours.

2 Let it cool and either freeze it for up to a month or keep it in the fridge for no more than 4 days, ready for use in a soup, risotto, gravy, chicken pie, curry…

❖**TIFF'S TIPS** I like to serve this with a very lovely creamy garlic mash. For a truly epic garlic mash, place a garlic bulb on an oven tray and roast at 200°C/400°F/Gas Mark 6 for 25 minutes. Then simply squeeze the soft cloves out of the skin, crush and whisk through a mash. I do buttered carrots and leeks alongside, or whatever is in season at the time.

COQ AU VIN ✪✪ SERVES 3–4

SHOPPING LIST

2–3 tablespoons olive oil

4 baby onions or shallots

3 garlic cloves, peeled and bruised

150g/5½oz bacon lardons
   (or use rashers, cut into
   squares)

2 chicken thighs

2 chicken legs

100g/3½oz baby mushrooms

25g/1oz butter

25g/1oz flour

400ml/14fl oz beef stock

250ml/9fl oz red wine

1 bunch thyme

salt and freshly ground black
   pepper

As the name of this classic French dish suggests, coq au vin is traditionally made using a cock bird, which you can order from your butcher. I use a regular supermarket chicken, however, and it works perfectly well.

The French make coq au vin with local wine, as it's a rustic dish and is usually made with easily available ingredients. I like it best when made with a Burgundy wine, probably because I always find I've got a spare half bottle left open.

Having jointed the chicken (see pages 112–13), I'm using the two legs and thighs for this. I always use the thighs and legs for coq au vin and actually for any chicken stew or casserole, as they perform much better when cooked slowly and at length, unlike chicken breasts, which tend to dry out.

1 Preheat the oven to 200°C/400°F/Gas Mark 6.

2 Take a frying pan and add 2 tablespoons of the oil. When hot, fry the baby onions and garlic cloves for 2–3 minutes until slightly golden. Then remove with a slotted spoon and place in a casserole dish.

3 Add the bacon to the frying pan and let it sizzle and cook for 2–3 minutes until golden. Transfer to the casserole dish.

4 If the pan is looking dry, add another tablespoon of oil and when hot add the chicken pieces. Season and cook for 3–4 minutes on both sides – the skin should be crispy and golden. Transfer to a casserole dish. Tip the mushrooms straight into the casserole without browning, this will allow them to soak up all the flavours from the casserole.

5 Melt the butter in the frying pan and add the flour. Cook for 1–2 minutes on low. This is a roux and will help to thicken the sauce.

6 Now pour in a bit of the stock – as much will fit in your pan – and whisk whilst the roux cooks through and begins to thicken. Transfer to the casserole dish and pour in the wine and any remaining stock that didn't fit in the frying pan.

7 Bung in the thyme bunch and cook in the oven for 1½ hours. Serve with mashed potatoes (see Tiff's Tip, opposite).

STICKY SPICY CHICKEN WINGS SERVES 2 ✪

SHOPPING LIST
2 tablespoons honey
2 tablespoons soy sauce
½ teaspoon red chilli flakes
½ teaspoon Chinese five spice
   powder
2 chicken wings

I did these once for a drinks party, just for a fun cheap nibble, and friends since request them all the time – my sister adores them! If you've jointed a chicken (see pages 112–13) this is a great way to use the two wings.

1 Preheat the oven to 200°C/400°F/Gas Mark 6.

2 Mix the honey and soy sauce together, then add the chilli flakes and Chinese five spice powder.

3 Smear over the wings, coating really well, and bake in the oven for 20 minutes.

4 Remove and serve with lots of napkins, as this is sticky work!

LEEK AND MUSHROOM STUFFED CHICKEN BREASTS SERVES 2 ✪ ✪

SHOPPING LIST
25g/1oz butter
2 spring onions
1–2 leeks, sliced
3–4 mushrooms, cut
   roughly into chunks
1 tablespoon white wine
   (optional)
3–4 tablespoons double
   cream
2 chicken breasts
black pepper

It's always those dishes that you don't plan that become a favourite. This is just the case with this lovely simple dish. I threw it together one night and it's become something I make time and time again. Having jointed your chicken, you have the two chicken breasts waiting to be dealt with – this is a perfect recipe for them.

1 Preheat the oven to 200°C/400°F/Gas Mark 6.

2 Melt the butter in a pan and then add the spring onions and fry gently for 1–2 minutes.

3 Up the heat slightly and add the leek slices and mushroom chunks. Cook on a gentle heat for 5 minutes until they are soft.

4 Add the white wine, if you're using it, and the double cream, and season really well with black pepper. Cook for a further 2–3 minutes and then set aside.

5 Take your chicken breasts and cut a pocket into them slightly to the top of the breast. Then take a spoon and stuff the pockets with the leek and mushroom mix.

6 Place the 2 breasts on a greaseproof oven tray and bake in the oven for 20 minutes, until the chicken shows no sign of pink juices when pierced with a sharp knife.

7 Remove from the oven, set aside for 3–4 minutes while you assemble your accompaniments and then serve.

❖**LEFTOVERS** If there's ever any stuffing left over I have to stop myself eating it straight from the pan, but it's fab on toast, or even with pasta. When you reheat it, put the mixture back in a pan and just add a little stock, cream or even a tablespoon of water to loosen it all up again. Leeks are in season autumn onwards; in the summer try it with peas.

❖**TIFF'S TIPS** For a truly comforting meal serve with a creamy mash, with cabbage on top and then the frikadeller on top of that.

❖**OPTIONAL EXTRAS** If you have any leftover cooked bacon, chuck it into the cabbage at the same time as the flour, milk and mustard. This works wonderfully.

SHOPPING LIST

250g/9oz pork mince
1 onion, chopped finely
1 egg, beaten
4 tablespoons plain flour
100g/3½oz butter
1 Savoy cabbage, shredded
100ml/3½fl oz milk
1 teaspoon mustard
salt and freshly ground black pepper

B'S DANISH FRIKADELLER SERVES 4 ✪✪

"My stepmother Betina is Danish and I've been fortunate enough to have been introduced to Scandinavian cuisine by her and my Norwegian best friend Ingrid. It's very much a no-frills approach. These tasty frikadeller, which are just like meatballs, instead of being served in tomato sauce are served instead with creamed cabbage. They're great little dumplings of delicious pork and are just bursting with flavour."

1 Mix the pork mince, onion and beaten egg together in a bowl until evenly combined. Then sprinkle in 2 tablespoons of the flour, and season really *really* well. If you want to check the seasoning, fry a teaspoon of the mixture, taste it and adapt it accordingly.

2 Shape the mixture into 2½cm/1inch dumplings. They should be slightly flatter than traditional meatballs and once you have made them all (this mixture makes about 14–16) place them on a tray in the fridge just to firm up whilst you prepare the cabbage.

3 Melt half the butter in a saucepan then add the shredded cabbage. Mix it round and let it soften for 4–5 minutes on a very low heat. Next add about half a cup of water. Leave it to cook gently for 5 minutes.

4 Add the remaining 2 tablespoons of flour and mix well, following swiftly with the milk and mustard. As the flour cooks, the sauce will gradually thicken. Season really well. Keep the cabbage on a very low heat while you cook the frikadeller.

5 Remove the tray of frikadeller from the fridge and heat the remaining butter in a frying pan. When it's melted and bubbling add the frikadeller and cook for 2–3 minutes on each side. Serve with the cabbage.

SHOPPING LIST

900ml/32fl oz fish stock
2 tablespoons olive oil
3 garlic cloves, peeled
  and crushed
1 large red onion, chopped finely
1 red chilli, deseeded and
  chopped finely
2 red peppers, deseeded and sliced
225g/8oz chorizo, sliced

1 teaspoon smoked paprika
450g/1lb paella rice, such as
  calasparra, bomba or bahia
3 tomatoes, quartered
pinch of sugar
1 glass white wine
6–8 saffron threads (optional)
200g/7oz small raw peeled prawns
150g/5½oz frozen peas

juice of 2 lemons
1 large bunch coriander,
  chopped roughly
lemon wedges, to serve
salt and freshly ground
  black pepper

PAELLA WITH PRAWNS AND CHORIZO

SERVES 6
★★★

"Paella is traditionally cooked in a paellera, which is a heavy shallow pan. I use a wok with two handles, which can just be brought straight to the table, but a shallow frying pan would work well too. When it comes to rice, if you fancy having a trawl through specialist food shops then try and get calasparra, bomba or bahia paella rice, which are what they use in Spain. Failing this, risotto rice also works well."

1 Place the fish stock in a pan and bring to a gentle simmer.

2 Heat the oil in a shallow wok or frying pan (of course use a paellera if you have one) and set over a medium heat.

3 Add the garlic, red onion, chilli and red pepper slices and sweat them gently for about 4 minutes.

4 Increase the heat a little and add the chorizo slices for 2 minutes. Now add the smoked paprika and rice. Mix round well, glazing the rice in the glorious rich rouge colour for a minute. Follow with the tomato quarters and season well, and add a pinch of sugar. Your tomatoes will soften and just gently add some delicate sweetness to the glorious flavours.

5 Now add the wine and let it reduce and absorb.

6 Gently pour the fish stock over the rice mixture, and add your gorgeous saffron threads, if using.

7 Leave the paella on a gentle simmer, and try to resist stirring it. Allow it to just gently absorb all the delicious liquid and flavours for about 10–15 minutes.

8 With 5 minutes of cooking to go, add the prawns and frozen peas to the rice, season and let the peas thaw out in the remaining liquid.

9 Add the lemon juice, taste and season accordingly. Remove from the heat, sprinkle with coriander and serve garnished with lemon wedges. Enjoy and *salud*...

❖TIFF'S TIPS Saffron is pretty expensive, as it's the dried stamens from the saffron crocus flowers. However, it imparts a delicious flavour and a deep rich colour. It is a fantastic marriage with seafood, so if you fancy investing in a pot you won't regret it, but leave it out if you prefer.

❖LEFTOVERS
Paella doesn't keep so well, as rice isn't recommended to be reheated, so just scoff it all, washed down with a glass of wine.

❖**TIFF'S TIPS** For an extra bit of flavour in the winter, fill your roasting tray with root vegetables, all chopped and coated in oil and piri piri sauce. This is a great dish in winter but is also wonderful done in the summer on the barbecue. Just eat it Portuguese style with some bread and salad, and washed down with some dry rosé.

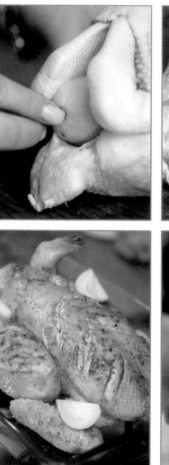

❖**LEFTOVERS** As this is slightly spicy, transform any leftovers into a curry with lots of turmeric, onions, coconut milk and stock. Take time to cook it down to intensify the flavours. Serve with basmati rice and lots of lime.

SHOPPING LIST

1.5kg/3lb 5oz free range or corn-fed chicken
1 lemon, halved
1 small onion, quartered
1 garlic bulb, halved
6 tablespoons piri piri sauce
6 tablespoons olive oil
salt and freshly ground black pepper

PORTUGUESE PIRI PIRI ROAST CHICKEN **SERVES 4** ✪✪

"I have been hugely fortunate to spend a great deal of my life in Portugal and have a huge love of the country, its people and its food. The Portuguese have massive characters and this echoes in their flamboyant cooking and loud flavours. *Piri piri* is their name for the bird's-eye chilli. They make this in every *churrasqueira* (chicken shack) and it's amazing."

1 Preheat the oven to 180°C/350°F/Gas Mark 4.

2 Place the chicken on a roasting tray and stuff the cavity with half the lemon, 2 onion quarters, and half the garlic bulb.

3 Then pour 2 tablespoons piri piri sauce and 2 tablespoons olive oil into the cavity. Season well with loads of salt and pepper.

4 Now cut 2 slits on each leg, each about 2½cm/1inch long. Then cut three more slits on each side of the breast.

5 Take the remaining piri piri sauce and really rub it well into the skin and slits. Do the same with 2 tablespoons of olive oil and lots of sea salt.

6 Heat a frying pan with the remaining 2 tablespoons olive oil. When hot, place the chicken in breast side down for 2 minutes and then turn over, sealing the skin and getting it crackingly crispy.

7 Now transfer into an oven dish, placing it legs down. Squeeze the remaining lemon half over the chicken, and tuck the remaining onion quarters and the garlic into the tray. Cook in the oven for 10 minutes, then reduce the heat to 140°C/275°F/Gas Mark 1.

8 Take the chicken out of the oven after 40 minutes, flip it over so its legs are up in the air and finish cooking like this for 35–45 minutes.

9 Check whether the chicken is cooked by piercing the thigh with a skewer or sharp knife – the juices should run clear. Leave it to rest, covered in foil, for 10 minutes. Serve carved on a big board with frites or rice and a big crispy salad. Just wonderful.

SHOPPING LIST

5 tablespoons plain flour
1 teaspoon red chilli flakes
850g/1lb 14oz beef, such as
  chuck or skirt, diced
3 tablespoons olive oil
1 onion, chopped finely
4 garlic cloves, peeled and
  bruised
200g/7oz pancetta or bacon
  lardons

250g/9oz button mushrooms
10 Chantenay carrots, left whole
300ml/10½fl oz beef stock
2 glasses red wine
bunch of thyme, rosemary or sage
250g/9oz puff pastry, thawed if frozen
1 egg, beaten
salt and freshly ground black pepper

NOT QUITE TOPLESS
BRAISED BEEF PIE SERVES 6 ✪✪

"Slow cooking brings out the best from cheaper cuts of meat. The general rule is that the parts of an animal that are worked the most tend to be cheaper, as the muscles will be tougher. This includes cuts like shank, brisket and chuck. I just love this with a flaky crisp puff pastry top, but it's not the healthiest option. A small circle of puff pastry is perhaps less sinful than an entire pastry lid."

1 Tip the flour into a shallow bowl, season well with salt and pepper and mix in the chilli flakes.

2 Dredge the beef chunks in the flour, coating well, then set aside.

3 Heat the olive oil in a heavy pan and when warm add the onion and garlic. Leave to soften for 1–2 minutes, then up the heat and add the pancetta. Fry for 3–4 minutes until the pancetta is crispy. The garlic and onion should be coloured and slightly crispy too.

4 Now add the beef and brown for 4–5 minutes, turning all the time on a medium heat.

5 Throw in your lovely button mushrooms and season well, following with the carrots.

6 Now pour over the beef stock and red wine. Bring to a boil and then simmer on a low heat for 1½ hours. Alternatively, cook in the oven at 160°C/325°F/Gas Mark 3 for 1½ hours.

7 Once cooked, remove from the heat to rest whilst you make your pastry puffs.

8 Heat the oven to 230°C/450°F/Gas Mark 8. Roll out the pastry until it's 1cm/½inch thick and then, using the base of a can as a template, cut 6 circles. Do a few extra if you have any leftover pastry. Brush a little egg onto the circles, and place on a baking tray in the hot oven for 5–8 minutes until puffed up and golden.

9 Remove from the oven and dish up the pie. Top each portion with a puff top.

❖**TIFF'S TIPS** I recently had leftovers of the beef mix and I shredded the beef cubes and transformed them into a bolognaise type sauce. Rich in flavour and utterly delicious with pasta like pappardelle. The pie is brilliant served with mash and seasonal veggies.

SHOPPING LIST

1 x 1½kg/3lb 5oz shoulder of pork, rolled and boned
3 tablespoons sunflower oil
2 tablespoons sea salt
3 large Bramley apples, halved and cored
2 tablespoons butter
6 sage leaves
1 tablespoon light brown sugar

SLOW ROASTED SHOULDER OF PORK WITH BAKED STUFFED APPLES SERVES 4–6 ✪✪✪

" Pork shoulder is sold in a huge range of sizes. For a great big roast, go to your butcher and ask for an on-the-bone joint of the shoulder, which will include some ribs and blade. Since it's the shoulder of the pig and therefore an overworked joint, the muscles are incredibly lean and therefore a prime cut for slow cooking. "

1 Preheat oven to 220°C/425°F/Gas Mark 7.

2 Take your pork and with a very sharp knife slit the fat lengthways at about 1cm/½inch intervals, not quite going all the way through. This is for the crackling and allows the fat to bubble up and form a cracking crackling. You can also ask your butcher to do this.

3 Massage the oil into the cracks of the pork and then rub the salt into the cracks too.

4 Set your pork on a roasting tray and place in the hot oven for the first 20 minutes, then remove from the oven and add a cup of water. This will give a steaming effect and keep the pork underside tender.

5 Place back in the oven at 160°C/325°F/Gas Mark 3 for 30 minutes.

6 Meanwhile prepare the apples. Take the halves and equally distribute the butter between them, pressing into the centre well that you have made. Top each apple half with a sage leaf.

7 Place the apple halves in the roasting tray alongside the pork. Spoon the excess juices over the apples and the pork, then sprinkle the sugar over the apples. Continue roasting for another hour.

8 Take the pork out of the oven and leave it to rest on a board.

9 Heat your grill to the highest setting. Remove the softening, slightly caramelised apples from the tray and set aside. When the grill is hot, place just the pork joint under there for 5 minutes, keeping a close eye, however, as it can catch and suddenly you'll have black crackling! When it's bubbled up and golden, remove.

10 Carve the joint into slices and serve with the apples.

❖**TIFF'S TIPS** Leaving the meat to rest lets all the muscles in the joint relax, which encourages the juices to run through the joint, promoting a full and fabulous flavour. I like to serve roast pork with crispy roast potatoes. You could roast them in the same tray as the apples and pork.

❖**OPTIONAL EXTRAS** I serve lovely baked apples with roast pork. In the summer, however, I swap the apples for some delicious roast peaches stuffed with lemon thyme.

❖**LEFTOVERS** Well, what's not to love about leftover lamb? The obvious use would be to make a shepherd's pie for the week ahead – just whizz up the lamb leftovers in a blender. This can also be done to make lamb lasagne (lamb ragù instead of beef).

❖**TIFF'S TIPS** This is utterly fantastic with potato gratin (see pages 130–31). If you do this then gravy is not necessarily vital. However, if you want to make a gravy, leave the lamb to rest on a board and use the juices in the roasting pan as the basis of your gravy. Put the pan on a medium heat and whisk round all the juices. Add 25g/1oz butter and 25g/1oz flour to form a roux and cook for 2 minutes. Then add a glass of wine and about 450ml–600ml/16–21fl oz beef, chicken or vegetable stock. Let it bubble for a few minutes to thicken, season well and serve. Easy as that!

SHOPPING LIST

2kg/4lb 8oz leg of lamb
4 garlic cloves, peeled and chopped roughly
4 rosemary sprigs
6 anchovies, chopped roughly
3 tablespoons olive oil
1 teaspoon balsamic vinegar
salt and freshly ground black pepper

SPIKED LEG OF LAMB WITH GARLIC AND ROSEMARY

SERVES 4–6 ✪✪✪

" Spring leg of lamb is incredibly lean and is best roasted and served pink. You can also ask your butcher to 'butterfly' the leg, which simply means removing the bone. In summer I like to marinade it in crème fraîche, garlic, mint and lemon, then cook it in the oven, finishing off on the barbecue. "

1 Preheat the oven to 180°C/350°F/Gas Mark 4 and place the lamb in a roasting tray.

2 Make 1cm/½ inch slits over the lamb, about 10 in total.

3 Press a bit of garlic into one of the slits followed by a little bit of rosemary and a little bit of anchovy. Repeat this for the rest of the slits, using all the garlic, rosemary and anchovies.

4 Rub well with oil and season all over. Spoon over the balsamic vinegar, which will add a slightly sweet tangy taste.

5 Roast in the hot oven for about 1 hour 20 minutes.

6 Remove the meat from the oven and allow it to rest for 10 minutes. I like my lamb slightly pink, but if you like it a little more done cook for a further 10–15 minutes.

7 Set on a board and carve at the table. You can refresh the lamb with a little more rosemary and garlic, if you like.

SHOPPING LIST

2kg/4lb 8oz waxy potatoes, peeled
50g/1¾oz butter
4 garlic cloves, peeled and sliced finely
350g/12oz mushrooms, sliced finely
3 sprigs rosemary, chopped
500ml/17fl oz double cream
150g/5½oz Cheddar cheese, grated
100g/3½oz Gruyère cheese, grated (optional)
salt and freshly ground black pepper

POTATO AND MUSHROOM CHEESY GRATIN ✪✪ SERVES 4–6

"Now if there is one recipe I get asked for all the time it's this. It's luscious, creamy, naughty and what's more it goes with so much. I sweep rosemary and mushrooms through the layers, which gives it extra depth of flavour. The secret is to choose waxy potatoes rather than floury, as they hold together much better."

1 Preheat the oven to 180°C/350°F/Gas Mark 4.

2 Using a sharp knife, slice the potatoes very thinly. Start by cutting a piece off the side of the potato to give it a flat edge on which to stand. This will make it much easier to slice. Do this with all the potatoes and then place in a saucepan of boiling water and cook for 5 minutes – no more, no less. Drain and run under cold water for a few minutes to stop the cooking process – you don't want overcooked slightly mashed potato slices.

3 Take a large ovenproof dish and rub half of the butter around the inside, add a little of the chopped garlic and add the first layer of potato slices.

4 Now sprinkle in a quarter of the mushroom slices and top with rosemary. Season really well with salt and pepper.

5 Now add the next layer of potatoes. Add a bit more garlic, season and add some more mushrooms and rosemary. Repeat this process until everything is used up. Four layers usually work for me.

6 Add the remaining butter on top of the potatoes and pour over the cream. It should fill up your dish.

7 Season again and top with the grated cheese. Cover the dish with foil and bake in the hot oven for 20 minutes. Remove the foil then return the gratin to the oven to brown for 15 minutes. The cheese will melt sumptuously.

❖**TIFF'S TIPS** This makes a delicious dinner on its own. Try adding some roasted vegetables or chicken leftovers between the layers. If serving with lamb, try folding chopped mint through it instead of rosemary.

❖**LEFTOVERS** If you have leftovers, add some seasonal veg and leftover chicken then mix it all round in an oven dish with a little cream or stock. Scatter with breadcrumbs and grated cheese, then place in the oven for 20 minutes for an easy tasty meal.

1 tablespoon sunflower oil
2 garlic cloves, crushed
1 onion, chopped finely
1 teaspoon red chilli flakes
1 teaspoon garam masala (not
  totally Thai but delish)
1 large butternut squash,
  peeled and diced
2 x 400ml/14fl oz cans coconut
  milk
360g/12oz basmati rice

1 teaspoon fish sauce
1 teaspoon granulated sugar or
  brown sugar
juice of 1 lemon
5–6 chicken breasts, sliced into
  strips
handful kaffir lime leaves
4 large tomatoes, quartered
25g/1oz butter
bunch of coriander, chopped
mango chutney, to serve

RED THAI CHICKEN AND SQUASH CURRY SERVES 6 ✪✪

❝Having been fortunate enough to have travelled extensively in Thailand and Asia, Thai curries are my first curry choice. I use garam masala in this recipe. This blend of Indian spices isn't strictly authentic to Thai curry but it works wonders, picking up the gentle flavours of the velvety butternut squash.❞

1 Heat the oil over a high heat in a wok or frying pan, then add the garlic, onion, chilli flakes and garam masala. Cook until soft and slightly coloured – about 2 minutes.

2 Add the squash and stir round to absorb all the flavours.

3 Pour in the coconut milk and reduce the heat to low-medium. Simmer for 10–15 minutes until the squash is soft.

4 Meanwhile bring a large pan of water to the boil and add the basmati rice. Cook for 7–10 minutes until soft. (I like my rice with a bit of bite to it.)

5 Add the fish sauce, sugar, lemon juice and chicken to the squash mixture. Simmer for 3 minutes and then add the kaffir lime leaves and tomatoes. Cook for a further 3–4 minutes.

6 Now drain the rice and place it back in the saucepan. Add the butter and season really well. Chop half the coriander and throw it into the rice.

7 Garnish the delicious steaming curry with the remaining coriander leaves and serve along with the rice and some yummy mango chutney. Naan bread and poppadoms also make great accompaniments – perfect for scooping up the curry.

❖**TIFF'S TIPS** I often find myself with leftover pitta bread and I substitute toasted pitta bread for the Naan and often tortilla chips for the poppadoms – a thriftier option and a fun alternative.

7

LET IT ALL GO

Right, let the belt out a notch, forget the diet and get stuck in. This is my naughty chapter full of delicious sweet treats. You'll feel ridiculously proud of yourself for baking and your friends will think you're a kitchen legend.

❖**TIFF'S TIPS** I urge you to freeze spare egg whites when making other recipes. You might think that you won't need to make meringues for ages, but I guarantee the minute you throw them away you'll wish you hadn't.

HOW TO MAKE MERINGUES
MINI PAVLOVAS WITH
SEASONAL BERRIES SERVES 4–6 ✿✿✿

SHOPPING LIST
3–4 egg whites
4 tablespoons sugar
250ml/9fl oz double cream
seasonal berries, such as
  blueberries, strawberries,
  raspberries, pomegranate
  seeds or passion fruit

The basic rule of whisking egg whites for meringues is to use a very clean and dry mixing bowl and whisk. A steel bowl is best but the main point is that your equipment should be totally clean or the egg white will not perform to its best. Meringues have to be cooked slowly. I prefer them crispy on top and then soft and gooey in the middle. The best way to achieve this is to cook them slowly and then, when done, turn the heat off and let them cool off in the oven – this gives them that softness inside. Make them ahead and they will keep in an airtight container for 4–5 days. Crisp on the outside yet fluffy within, a meringue is simply cooked whisked egg white. You can add sugar and vinegar to make the white different in ways that I will explain later, but the essential white fluffiness of a meringue is simply due to egg whites. There are hardly any calories at all in a meringue, which is nice and something I always think of happily when I eat them. The fact they are usually filled with whipped cream and all sorts of other naughties is another matter entirely.

1 Preheat the oven to 140°C/275°F/Gas Mark 1.

2 Break the egg whites into a large clean bowl and using an electric whisk or a hand held whisk (although this will take time and a lot of elbow grease) begin whisking. When they start to foam, gradually add the sugar, bit by bit.

3 Keep whisking until they form stiff peaks. The sugar will not only make them delicious but also make the egg white rich and velvety.

4 Line a baking tray with greaseproof paper. I use a dab of the whisked egg white to stick the corners of the paper to the baking tray. Then use a tablespoon to spoon on the whites. Flatten each dollop a little to create a nest-like shape about 2½cm/1 inch wide and repeat until you have used all the mixture.

5 Place in the oven and cook for 35–40 minutes until they are hard. Turn off the oven and let the meringues cool inside it while you whisk the cream.

6 Pour the double cream into a bowl and whisk until it's stiff.

7 Place the meringue nests on a serving plate and top each one with a tablespoon of cream and some fruit.

138 LET IT ALL GO

MY PINK AND GIRLY MERINGUE KISSES SERVES 4–6 ✪✪✪

SHOPPING LIST
3–4 egg whites
4 tablespoons sugar
3 tablespoons pink food
  colouring (can also use blue,
  red, etc.)
250ml/9fl oz double cream

Unbelievably cute, you can of course make these meringues any colour you like. I make this pink version when the girls are over. It always seems that people are amazed you can make coloured meringues.

1 Preheat the oven to 140°C/275°F/Gas Mark 1.

2 Break the egg whites into a large clean bowl and using an electric whisk or a hand held whisk (although this will take time and a lot of elbow grease) begin whisking the egg whites. When they start to foam, gradually add the sugar, bit by bit.

3 Keep whisking until the whites form stiff peaks, then very carefully fold in the pink colouring. Don't mix it in completely, though, as you want to achieve a marbled effect.

4 Line a baking tray with greaseproof paper, then use a tablespoon to spoon on the meringue mixture. Make sure they have good peaks on them.

5 Place in the oven and cook for 35–40 minutes. Then turn off the oven and let the meringues cool inside it while you whisk the cream.

6 Pour the double cream into a bowl and whisk until it's stiff. Spoon onto a serving plate and top with a pile of meringue kisses.

DIY ETON MESS SERVES 4–6 ✪✪✪

SHOPPING LIST
6 meringue nests or kisses
  (see pages 136–37 and above),
  crumbled
500ml/17fl oz double cream,
  whipped
150g/5½oz mini marshmallows
100g/3½oz seasonal berries,
  such as blueberries,
  strawberries or pomegranate
  seeds
sugar cake decorations

Instead of the traditional Eton mess recipe (one of my favourite puddings ever), it's fun to create all the elements and place them on the table so your guests can create their own. I've tried this when I've had people round and it was hilarious, somewhere between dessert and a kids' tea party. I always talk about ice breakers and getting people involved some way, and this is the perfect example.

1 Place all the ingredients in separate bowls and give everyone either an ice cream sundae glass, a large wine glass or a bowl.

2 Put all the bowls on the table and simply and superbly let everyone build their own combination of meringue, whipped cream, marshmallows, berries and sugar cake decorations.

SHOPPING LIST

200g/7oz mixed berries, such as raspberries, strawberries and blueberries, fresh or frozen

2 tablespoons sugar

250g/9oz sponge cake or Madeira cake, thickly sliced

3 tablespoons strawberry or raspberry jam

3 tablespoons sparkling wine or sherry (optional)

150g/5½oz readymade custard

300ml/10½fl oz double cream

2 tablespoons hundreds and thousands, to decorate (optional)

2 tablespoons flaked almonds, to decorate (optional)

punnet of raspberries, to decorate (optional)

TIFF'S RETRO TRIFLE
SERVES 4 ✪✪

"Retro dishes like trifle are slowly but surely making their way back onto restaurant menus. Guaranteed to spark happy childhood memories, there are so many versions of this British classic. Some have a gelatine base while others, like mine, are more simple. Brilliant to serve at Christmas, it's also perfect to use up leftover cream sponge and of course alcohol."

1 If you are using frozen berries (which I would recommend if you are not in the midst of summer) then tip them into a saucepan and add enough water so they are just covered. Add the sugar and place on the heat to bring to a simmer.

2 Simmer for 5 minutes until soft, then set aside. If you're using fresh fruit, however, you won't need to add the sugar or indeed simmer the fruit.

3 Now take half your cake slices (this is a fantastic way to use up sponge cake if you have leftover bits). Add a smidge of jam and place in a large serving bowl, jam side up. (If you're using individual sundae glasses then cut your sponge pieces to fit.)

4 Add a little fizz or sherry next, but feel free to leave it out if you wish.

5 Take a slotted spoon and spoon in half the fruit with about 1–2 tablespoons of juice.

6 Now repeat the sponge step, layering the remaining sponge slices jam side up on top of the first batch of fruit. Cover with the remaining fruit and 1–2 tablespoons of the sugary juice.

7 Pour the custard over the top and place in the fridge.

8 Meanwhile whisk the cream in a good clean bowl using either a hand whisk or an electric whisk. Whisk until the cream is stiff.

9 Remove the trifle from the fridge and either dollop the cream on top or, for a smarter effect, use a piping bag to pipe it on. Serve chilled.

❖**TIFF'S TIPS** This is a savvy dinner party dish because you can make it in the morning and leave it to chill in the fridge all day until you're ready. I also quite like to add some marshmallows to the cream for a really fun twist!

❖**OPTIONAL EXTRAS** For a full-on retro experience, top your trifle with outrageous sprinkles of hundreds and thousands or flaked almonds. Or arrange raspberries on top of the trifle and douse with icing sugar.

SHOPPING LIST

250g/9oz good quality white chocolate, chopped

80ml/2½fl oz milk

1 teaspoon natural vanilla extract

3 eggs, separated

375ml/13fl oz double cream

seasonal fruit such as pomegranate seeds, raspberries,
    strawberries or blackberries

mint sprigs, to garnish

WHITE CHOCOLATE AND VANILLA MOUSSE WITH SEASONAL FRUITS

MAKES 4–6 INDIVIDUAL MOUSSES ✪✪✪

"These bite-size mousses with fresh fruit nestled on top just scream 'eat me'. I'm a big fan of puddings served in wine glasses, flutes or espresso cups; somehow they just seem far more entertaining. These are great if you need to impress and can be made in advance, ready to whip out of the fridge."

1 Put the chocolate, milk and vanilla extract in a heatproof bowl over a saucepan of simmering water, making sure that the bowl does not touch the water. Heat until the chocolate is just melted, stirring regularly.

2 Remove the bowl from the heat and allow to cool for 5 minutes, then add the egg yolks, beating well after each addition.

3 Whip the cream in a bowl until soft peaks form, then fold through the chocolate mixture until just combined.

4 Whisk the egg whites in a large, dry bowl until soft peaks form. Using a large metal spoon, carefully fold into the chocolate mixture in two batches.

5 Divide the mousse between your glasses, ramekins or coffee cups. Place in the fridge to chill for 2–3 hours.

6 Arrange the fruit on top of the set mousse (I've used pomegranate seeds here) and garnish with fresh mint leaves.

❖**TIFF'S TIPS** When you whisk egg white it injects air into the protein in the white, which creates a foam. This takes about 5 minutes using a hand-held whisk, so when you fold the whites into the chocolate take real care not to beat out all the air you have laboriously whipped in.

❖**OPTIONAL EXTRAS**
You could make a raspberry coulis by pressing a handful of raspberries through a sieve and then folding the resulting brilliant bright coulis through the mousse.

❖**TIFF'S TIPS** This will keep for up to a month in the freezer, and for extra decadence drizzle more chocolate sauce over the top. It's also nice to fold through some blueberries.

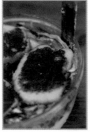

SHOPPING LIST

350g/12oz Madeira cake or plain sponge, thickly sliced
2–3 tablespoons chocolate spread
250g/9oz plain chocolate, broken into chunks
50g/1¾oz butter
100g/3½oz chocolate chips
500ml/17fl oz double cream
1 teaspoon vanilla essence
3 tablespoons cocoa powder
chocolate chips, to decorate
sparklers, to decorate

SPARKLY CHOCOLATE BOMBE SERVES 4–6 ✪✪✪

This is my version of an over-the-top chocolate trifle. I love to do it as a variation of a birthday cake, or serve it at Christmas – either way it's fun to add sparklers or candles. This recipe is very simple and requires no oven, so it's just the assembly that takes a little time. Make it in the morning, as it needs time to set properly. If you want to spice it up then add a little booze – I've added vodka, cava and even sherry to it.

1 Take the Madeira cake pieces and spread them with chocolate spread for extra naughtiness. Set aside.

2 Put the chocolate and butter in a mixing bowl and place on a saucepan of simmering water. Make sure the water doesn't touch the base of the bowl, however. Melt slowly for about 5 minutes and then remove the bowl from the pan and leave to cool.

3 Meanwhile place a third of the Madeira chocolate slices on the bottom of a 1litre/35fl oz pudding bowl – chocolate side up.

4 Sprinkle over about a tablespoon of chocolate chips and then drizzle with some of the chocolate sauce.

5 In a mixing bowl whisk half the cream until thick and then spoon half of it over the chocolate sponge mixture.

6 Repeat the process with the sponge (chocolate side up), then the chocolate sauce, now the choc chips and then cream again, and finish with a layer of sponge.

7 Place a heavy plate on top of the bowl and put it all in the fridge for an hour. After an hour place in the freezer for at least 4 hours.

8 On removal from the freezer leave for about 5 minutes to thaw a little. Meanwhile, whisk the rest of the cream and the vanilla essence, adding in the cocoa powder bit by bit.

9 Run a knife round the side of the pudding to free it up. Carefully place the bombe upside down on a serving plate and push it out gently. Now spread with the chocolate cream and garnish with chocolate chips and sparklers.

SHOPPING LIST

300g/10½oz butter, softened
150g/5½oz caster sugar
150g/5½oz soft brown sugar
1 teaspoon cinnamon (optional)
100g/3½oz walnuts, chopped
  finely
70g/2½oz carrots, peeled and
  grated (about 1 large carrot)
3–4 tablespoons raisins
4 large eggs, beaten

300g/10½oz plain flour
3 teaspoons baking powder
8 walnut halves, to decorate

Icing:
250g/9oz butter, softened
275g/9¾oz icing sugar
2–3 tablespoons cocoa
1 teaspoon vanilla essence

CARROT AND WALNUT CAKE WITH CREAM ICING SERVES 6–8 ★★

" A few years ago my grandmother made me some carrot cake and it was a revolutionary moment. I was hooked from that moment on – her cake was sweet, fluffy and light so it was straight back to my kitchen and with walnuts and carrots being thrown around the kitchen I had a go myself. I love the raisins in it, as they give a cake that gooey texture I find so good. "

1 Preheat the oven to 180°C/350°F/Gas Mark 4.

2 Grease and line a 22cm/9inch springform circular cake tin (I also like to make this in a heart-shaped tin).

3 Beat the butter in a large bowl until really soft. Now add the caster and soft brown sugar and mix well until they form a smooth and creamy mixture.

4 Sprinkle over the cinnamon, if using, add the walnuts, grated carrots and raisins and beat well until all is combined.

5 Now add the beaten eggs and mix well. When smooth, sift the flour and baking powder in bit by bit, mixing all the time.

6 The mixture will become tougher and thicker as you mix in the flour. When it's all combined and smooth, tip it into the cake tin and bake in the oven for 30–35 minutes. To check whether it's done, insert a skewer into the cooked cake – it should come out clean.

7 Remove the cake from the oven, turn out onto a wire rack and allow to cool.

8 Meanwhile make the icing. Cream the butter until smooth and sift in the icing sugar and cocoa powder. Beat until really smooth, then add the vanilla essence and mix again.

9 Dollop the icing on top of the cake. Dip a palette knife or just a normal knife into a mug of hot water. Use the hot wet knife to smooth the icing over the cake. This will give it a lovely glossy finish.

10 Decorate the cake with walnuts and serve.

❖**TIFF'S TIPS** I sometimes remove the carrots and add 3–4 tablespoons instant coffee, which really works brilliantly with the dark buttery walnuts.

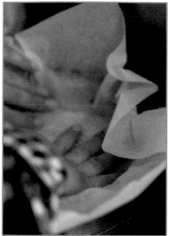

❖**LEFTOVERS** Keep your cake in an airtight tin for up to 5 days.

SHOPPING LIST

200g/7oz self-raising flour
2 tablespoons cocoa powder
1 teaspoon bicarbonate of soda
½ teaspoon salt
140ml/4½fl oz milk
3 tablespoons soured cream
1½ teaspoons white wine vinegar
1 teaspoon vanilla essence
1½ tablespoons red food colouring

100g/3½oz butter
210g/7½oz caster sugar
1 egg
1 punnet blueberries

Cream cheese frosting:
110g/3¾oz butter, softened
270g/9¾oz icing sugar
150g/5½oz cream cheese

½ teaspoon vanilla essence (optional)
cherries, to decorate (optional)

14 cupcake cases

MY RED VELVET AMERICAN CUPCAKES WITH BLUEBERRIES MAKES 14 ✪✪

"Red velvet cake is a hugely popular American cake, made famous by the Waldorf Astoria hotel in New York. Don't be put off by the addition of vinegar and soured cream – trust me, they taste sublime. They are there to achieve a rich, slightly tart flavour. If you want to use buttermilk, then substitute it for the milk and soured cream."

1 Preheat the oven to 180°C/350°F/Gas Mark 4.

2 Sift the flour, cocoa, bicarbonate of soda and salt into a bowl.

3 Mix together the milk, soured cream, white wine vinegar, vanilla essence and food colouring.

4 Now take a large mixing bowl and cream the butter until soft, then beat in the caster sugar until smooth. Add the egg and beat thoroughly until combined.

5 Add half the dry flour mixture to the creamed butter and mix well. Next add half the red milky liquid mix and mix well again. Repeat this step with the remaining flour and remaining milk mixture. Fold in the blueberries.

6 Place the cupcake cases on a baking tray and spoon a tablespoon of mixture into each case.

7 Place in the preheated oven for 20 minutes until risen and slightly firm to touch.

8 Meanwhile make the frosting. Take a mixing bowl and cream the soft butter until smooth. Sift the icing sugar into the bowl and mix well. Now fold in the cream cheese and add the vanilla essence, if you're using it. It should be delicious, light and fluffy.

9 Remove your cupcakes from the oven and leave them for about 20 minutes to cool. Set your icing aside in a cool dry place.

10 Smear a teaspoon of icing over each cupcake, then decorate with fresh cherries.

❖TIFF'S TIPS Dip a palette knife or a normal knife in a jug of hot water as you spread the icing. This gives a very smooth finish.

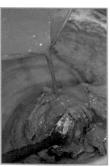

❖LEFTOVERS These cupcakes can be kept in an airtight tin for up to 5 days.

❖**TIFF'S TIPS** Add some chopped walnuts if you like, and even some white chocolate chips for extra decadence.

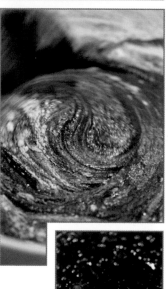

❖**LEFTOVERS** The brownies can be kept for up to 5 days if stored in an airtight container.

SHOPPING LIST

300g/10½oz butter
200g/7oz dark chocolate
5 large eggs
450g/1lb caster sugar
200g/7oz plain flour
1 teaspoon salt
100g/3½oz chocolate chips
2 tablespoons raisins
250g/9oz dried cherries or cranberries

CHERRY CHOCOLATE BROWNIES ✪✪ MAKES 18–20

"Forget chocolate brownies, these, introduced to me by friend Cress' mum, Bryony, are revolutionary. The chewy gooey dried cherries make them impossible to put down. Add nuts if you wish, but for me this is the ultimate treat. Great as edible presents too."

1 Preheat the oven to 180°C/350°F/Gas Mark 4.

2 Grease your baking tin and line with greaseproof paper. I use a tin 34 x 25cm/13½ x 10inches and about 5cm/2inches deep.

3 Bring a pan of water to the boil, place a heatproof bowl over the water (make sure it isn't touching the simmering water) and put in the dark chocolate and butter. Melt until smooth and creamy. Set aside and leave to cool for about 5 minutes.

4 Meanwhile whisk the eggs and then beat in the sugar until thick and creamy.

5 Now take the cooled butter and choc mixture and gently fold into the egg mixture.

6 Sieve the flour and salt. Fold into the mixture until smooth. Then fold in the chocolate chips.

7 Now stir in the raisins and cherries or cranberries along with the chocolate chips. Mix again until smooth.

8 Spoon the mixture into your tin and place in the oven for 20–30 minutes. When done it should have a slightly cracked top but hopefully will be deliciously gooey inside!

9 Leave to cool in the tin and then cut into squares as big or small as you like.

❖**TIFF'S TIPS** Serve with butter or the traditional way with whipped or clotted cream and a heavenly strawberry jam. If you can resist them, scones can be kept for 3 days in an airtight container.

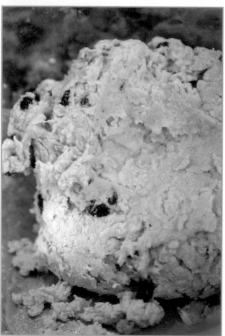

SHOPPING LIST

500g/1lb 2oz self-raising flour
1 teaspoon salt
60g/2¼oz caster sugar
80g/2¾oz butter, cold and diced
1 medium egg, beaten
200ml/7fl oz milk
150g/5½oz raisins

Glaze:

2 tablespoons milk
4 tablespoons sugar

SCONES ✪✪ MAKES 10

❝Scones are fast bread in a way; you make the dough but miraculously they're ready in about 10 minutes, they're super simple to make and you need just a few ingredients for them. I love fruit scones and fill mine with raisins. Alternatively, you could make a savoury version by adding cheese or lots of chopped herbs. They're at their absolute best when still warm from the oven.❞

1 Preheat the oven to 180°C/350°F/Gas Mark 4.

2 Sieve the flour, salt and sugar into a large mixing bowl. Mix well and then add the butter. Rub the butter into the flour mixture making fine breadcrumbs. Your butter must be cold for this.

3 Add the beaten egg to the milk, then stir in the raisins.

4 Make a well in the flour mixture and gradually mix in the liquid until you get a smooth dough.

5 Knead for a minute in the bowl and then scatter some flour onto your work surface and tip out your beautiful dough.

6 Take a rolling pin and roll out the dough until it's about 4cm/1½in thick. Using a 5cm/2in cutter, cut out the rounds and place them on a floured baking tray. You will need to reroll the dough to use it all.

7 Brush with milk and sprinkle with sugar to glaze the scones.

8 Place in the hot oven for 10–12 minutes until risen and golden.

100g/3½oz salted butter
50g/1¾oz sugar
180g/6oz plain flour
3 tablespoons granulated sugar,
    for sprinkling

SHORTBREAD ✪ MAKES 10 SLICES

"If you don't fancy yourself a dab hand at baking then shortbread is for you. There are only three ingredients involved and it can be ready in a flash."

1 Cream the soft butter in a bowl until smooth, then stir in the sugar until all combined.

2 Add the flour, and using your hands, get stuck in and mix well. Form a ball of dough.

3 Dust some flour over your work surface and roll out the pastry. Take a cutter, round, heart-shaped, star-shaped, and cut. Or just cut it into squares or fingers.

4 Place a layer of greaseproof paper on a baking tray and add the shortbread. Cook for 10 minutes until golden.

5 Remove from the oven and sprinkle with granulated sugar.

❖**TIFF'S TIPS** Try adding ½ teaspoon vanilla essence to the mixture to give the shortbread a little extra sweetness.

❖**LEFTOVERS** Spoon a teaspoon of whipped cream onto a shortbread heart and then layer another one on top. Finish with a little more cream and some chopped strawberries.

INDEX

ACKNOWLEDGEMENTS

" Writing this book has been a blast and I've loved every minute of it. There are so many people who enable it all to happen, and I'm incredibly lucky that the team are so unbelievably talented.

Primarily I would like to thank everyone at Quadrille Publishing for their continuing faith and support in me and in this book. Anne Furniss, it seems a lifetime ago we first met when I was fresh out of uni and I'm so grateful for all you have given me in these two books, without you it wouldn't be as wonderful as it all is, so thank you. Helen Lewis, thank you for enabling this book in its design and putting together a formidable team in the form of Katherine Case and Rob Streeter. Katherine, wow what fun we had the second time round shooting this book, singing and eating; you're amazingly talented and I'm so grateful for your beautiful designs and brilliant ideas. Your vision for this book has been flawless. Rob Streeter – I am honoured that mine was your first book you photographed but I do not think it will be your last as the pictures are phenomenal. Mark McGinlay in publicity, thank you so much for all your ongoing support and enthusiasm in this project as well as your awesome work on the first book. Katey Mackenzie, thank you so much for your tireless work getting me on track, keeping me on track and for all your efforts making this book what it is. It has been brilliant to work with you again and I cannot thank you enough.

Heather Holden Brown and Elly James you are always inspiring me and pushing me forward and I thank you both so much for all your support, couldn't have got here without you so I'm hugely grateful. Rosemary Melbourne, thank you for everything. Where to start? All the day-to-day activities, looking after me and enabling me to make the most of some fantastic opportunities, look forward to much more.

My first flat housemate, Lottie, for putting up with all the cooking and chaos during the shoots and writing, it's a pleasure and a joy living with you. And little Woody, thanks for being the purrrrfect furry model in the book. All my friends, thank you for always being supportive and visiting me at shows and events. Ingrid and Lara, my girls, thank you for all your ideas and help with everything and anything. Barny, thank you for showing such an interest in food and I love the way you have started to cook. Vicks you're a star – so much love and start cooking...

B, thanks for the lovely recipes including the fab frikadellers. Oma you are a fantastic support and I'm so lucky to have such a brilliant grandmother, who instilled so much of my passion in food in me from such a young age. Guy, you're the best person to share this all with and I just love everything we do together. Every day brings so much more excitement. Kamillie, I love cooking with you and thank you for being such an interested and wonderful little sister. George, you're a dreadful cook but a glorious and incredible sister.

Finally, I'm so fortunate to have two gloriously incredible parents, whom I adore. Papa, thank you for all the wonderful help with the flat, for being such a fantastic father and a best friend. Mummy, it's been a mad year and I just couldn't do any of this without you. You're the most thoughtful person I know and always have my best needs at heart, enabling and supporting me. "